MAGIC EYE®

Beyond 3D:
Improve Your Vision with Magic Eye

by Magic Eye, Inc., & Marc Grossman, O.D., L.Ac.

Andrews McMeel
PUBLISHING®

Andrews McMeel Publishing
a division of Andrews McMeel Universal
1130 Walnut Street, Kansas City, Missouri 64106

www.andrewsmcmeel.com

23 24 25 26 27 WKT 26 25 24 23 22

ISBN: 978-0-7407-4527-0

Director and Project Coordinator: Cheri Smith

Magic Eye 3D Images Creators: Cheri Smith, Dawn Zimiles, and Ron Labbe

Book Design and Production: Cheri Smith, Dawn Zimiles, Susan Seed, and Shirl Roccapriore

Writers: Marc Grossman, O.D., L.Ac., and Cheri Smith

Editors: Shira Shaiman, Peter Bissonette, Lynn McKenna, John Schrimpf, Linda Davis, Cynthia Poor, and Linda Luongo

Disclaimer:
The information contained in this book is intended to be educational and entertaining and is not for diagnosis, prescription, or treatment of any eye conditions or disease or any health disorder whatsoever. This information should not replace competent optometric or medical care. The authors are in no way liable for any use or misuse of this material. It needs to be emphasized, however, that current understanding of vision and the brain is still in many ways a mystery to science. Many of the theories presented in this book are far from being fully researched. Our wish is that these ideas and experiences will inspire further research to help unlock the mystery of how vision and the brain work.

Vision Works, Inc., is a Web site company cocreated by Dr. Grossman, O.D., L.Ac.

www.visionworksusa.com

ATTENTION: SCHOOLS AND BUSINESSES

Magic Eye® Images are available for educational, business, or sales promotional use. For information, please e-mail sales@magiceye.com, or contact us at:

Magic Eye, Inc., P.O. Box 1986, Provincetown, MA 02657
www.magiceye.com

Andrews McMeel books are available at quantity discounts with bulk purchase for educational, business, or sales promotional use. For information, please e-mail the Andrews McMeel Publishing Special Sales Department: sales@amuniversal.com.

Contents

History of Magic Eye & Beyond 3D

History of Magic Eye 3D Illusions

How did we invent this amazing illusion? The basic concept has existed for many years. In 1959, Dr. Bella Julesz was the first to use two computer-generated 3D images made up of randomly placed dots to study depth perception in human beings. The two images were viewed side by side. Because the dot pictures did not contain any other information like color or shapes, he could be sure that when his subject saw the picture, it was 3D only.

In 1979, Christopher Tyler, Ph.D., a student of Dr. Julesz, assisted by computer programmer Maureen Clarke, discovered that the offset scheme could be applied to a single image. This was the birth of the black-and-white single-image random-dot stereogram.

In 1991, programmer Tom Baccei and artist Cheri Smith collaborated to create 3D art based on improvements to the research of Julesz, Tyler, and Clarke. Baccei and Smith invented a new, sophisticated full-color stereogram program in combination with state-of-the-art 3D modeling software and colorful art techniques and developed a totally new patented art form . . . MAGIC EYE®!

Magic Eye books ignited the worldwide stereogram explosion of the 1990s, breaking best-seller list records around the world. Every week, from 1991 and into the millennium, millions of people literally *stare* at our images on books, posters, calendars, advertisements, and other retail products, as well as our syndicated newspaper feature.

Magic Eye images were first released by N.E. Thing Enterprises, which reorganized in 1996 as Magic Eye Inc. Cheri Smith is the president and creative director of Magic Eye Inc.

History of Beyond 3D

When I viewed my first black-and-white single-image random-dot stereogram, I was amazed. I immediately wanted to know how my eyes could perceive this incredible illusion, what type of "altered state" it seemed to place me into, and most importantly, how could I create them!

Since 1991, we have received thousands of letters and e-mails asking some of the same questions I initially had. We also received just as much correspondence *informing us* of experiences people were having as a result of viewing Magic Eye images. Some people felt happy or noticeably elated by viewing the images. Others felt calm to serene. Many felt relief by "escaping into" the 3D images. People reported of vision improvement, as well as stress and pain reduction.

In order to view Magic Eye images, you need vision in both eyes. Your eyes need to work together as a focused team. As a result, the left and right sides of your brain are stimulated more while viewing a Magic Eye image. Because of this we became very popular with anyone teaching or studying "whole mind" or "brain synchronization" types of practices, including vision therapy, accelerated learning, speed reading, stress management, pain management, meditation, yoga, "expanding your mind," "accessing presence," developing your intuition, even learning to see auras. These practices focus on inducing the same state you may induce by viewing Magic Eye images.

Magic Eye images are also being used as educational tools in schools. Our images "appear" in many science and psychology school textbooks. Thousands of students use Magic Eye as a topic for papers and projects. In addition, many teachers report they use Magic Eye images to focus or inspire students. Guidance counselors, on the other hand, hang Magic Eye images in their waiting rooms to "calm" students.

I am thrilled to present *Magic Eye Beyond 3D*. I would like to take this opportunity to thank everyone who contributed to this project. This book is dedicated to everyone who enjoys Magic Eye images for *any* reason. *Beyond 3D* will touch on many of the topics I have mentioned above and hopefully, after reading and *viewing* this book, you will also *know* why Magic Eye images truly are *magic*.

~Cheri Smith, president, Magic Eye Inc.

www.magiceye.com

Beyond 3D & Vision

As an optometrist, I became very excited when Magic Eye images were created over ten years ago. Not only were they fun, they also could produce incredible changes in both people's vision and in the way they could relate to the world. Magic Eye images have since become a major part of my vision therapy program in helping people improve their vision and their lives.

A Magic Eye image is an enhanced version of what is scientifically called a "black-and-white single-image random-dot stereogram." Abbreviated it is referred to as a "stereogram." A stereogram is a type of image that allows you to see a second three-dimensional image contained in the first picture without special equipment. While you don't need a funny pair of glasses to see the Magic Eye hidden 3D images, you do need to train your eyes to see in a new way. This new way of seeing involves both your mind and your eyes as you learn to see the world with "soft eyes."

Miyamoto Musashi, the legendary 17th-century swordsman, describes this soft-focused vision in his classic exposition on sword-fighting, *The Book of Five Rings.* Musashi describes two types of vision. One he calls *ken,* an observation of surface appearances and external movement. The other is *kan,* the deeper seeing into the essence of things, which the samurai must master to become a skilled warrior. Using the peripheral vision of kan, Musashi explains, a warrior can quickly spot an enemy and detect an impending attack before it happens.

The kan way of seeing has many other benefits outside of the martial arts: It can help us stay calm, improve concentration, creativity, intuition, and our ability to expand our visual field. Kan is also the type of vision we use to see Magic Eye 3D hidden images.

Kan seeing may sound like a mysterious skill, but it actually has a simple physiological explanation. The retina of the eye can be divided into two parts: One part is called the fovea, which is densely packed with cells called cones. The cones bring images into a hard focus that is clear, logical, and related to an analytical way of looking at the world. Each cone has a single nerve that connects to the brain, and information that enters the fovea is processed by the conscious mind. The second part of the retina is its periphery, which houses cells called rods. Even though several hundred rods connect to the same nerve, these cells are very sensitive. In fact, they can detect a single star thousands of miles a way. In plain English, the cones allow us to focus very closely on an object—such as an individual leaf—while the rods give us more expanded peripheral vision—we can see the forest.

With Magic Eye—Musashi's kan way of seeing—you are trying to achieve a balance between the rod vision and the cone vision, using more of your peripheral vision than normal. This relaxes our hard-focus analytical way of seeing and softens our gaze to take in a more expanded peripheral visual field. And since the periphery of our visual field is processed mostly by the subconscious mind, this soft focus gaze creates a more emotional and intuitive way of seeing the world.

This soft focus allows the hidden images from the Magic Eye pictures to appear. As that image gets put into context, it becomes more than just an "observation"; it becomes an "experience"!

As this visual world changes in front of us we become more open to "seeing" the world as a whole new adventure.

Of all our senses—touch, taste, smell, hearing, and sight—vision is our most developed. It is our dominant sense and the means by which the average person receives the vast majority of their information and education. It has been shown that nearly 85 percent of all of the information that we gather in a lifetime is taken into our minds through our eyes.

The information that we take in our eyes is the raw material from which we create our own sense of reality. The context that is based upon past experience determines our behavior in present circumstances. Therefore, the quality of our vision, how well and truly we are seeing, to a great extent determines the quality of our personal reality and shapes how we live our lives.

Perhaps even more importantly, our eyes are the only organs of our bodies that are actually outgrowths of our brain. The eye's retina is, in reality, a specialized form of brain tissue. This makes the interconnection and interrelationship between our eyes and our brain the most profound organic relationship in our body, in our being. It means that the information taken in by the eye is processed by the brain differently—more deeply and completely, in fact—than is the information that we receive through all our other senses.

What makes the Magic Eye image such a special experience is that it exists on two levels of reality. One is the obvious surface level of a repeating pattern of color, but there is also a deeper, hidden level.

The surface level of some Magic Eye images appear to be random splashes of color. For other images, however, the surface can be a rigidly repeated pattern that is highly organized and seems to be complete in itself. No matter what the surface appearance of the image, there is always a deeper level. The deeper level is the "real" reality of the Magic Eye 3D image. The surface is only a distraction from what is hidden. When the hidden image is found then the real meaning and experience of the Magic Eye 3D image occurs. If the deeper level is not seen then the essential experience is lost.

In my opinion, the true experience of viewing a Magic Eye image is the ability to see what is invisible—at least, what is not readily visible to the unseeing eye. The discovery of the hidden image is a dynamic event that changes us from passive observers of a picture to active participants in a new experience of seeing. As we change our perceptions of what we can and cannot see, we can become more open to viewing the world as a whole new adventure. As a metaphor of life, you could say that the sudden revelation of the hidden image helps us expand our vision, our sense of possibility, to include what we didn't see previously. What else can we see that we don't know we can see?

I want to assure you that like most aspects of life, vision is not static. Even if you've worn glasses for the last 20 years, it may be possible to improve your vision. It is our wish that viewing Magic Eye images will help you enhance your precious gift of sight.

Even if you view the Magic Eye images only for fun, in the process you just may discover deeper layers of reality that lie beyond the surface. But don't just take my word for it. Seeing is believing.

Preparing for Vision Exercises

Breathe. Many people naturally hold their breath when they concentrate on a visual task. To get the greatest benefit out of the Magic Eye images, however, it is important to keep breathing. Breathing helps us stay relaxed, which is a vital part of keeping our eyes working at their optimal potential.

Blink. This may seem obvious, but you'd be surprised by the number of people who forget to blink when they are looking at something. Avoid staring or fixing your eyes while you look at the images. Remember, blinking is essential for eye health. It soothes, moisturizes, and relaxes the eyes.

Relax. Try to enjoy yourself as you look for the hidden images. Be aware not to hold tension in your neck, shoulders, and jaw. If you feel any increased stress in those areas, take a break from the images to breathe or palm your eyes (see description at right).

Smile. You will be amazed at how important this is. Make sure you smile with your eyes as well as your mouth. Smiling reduces the tension in your eyes and relaxes your whole body.

Palming to Reduce Eye Stress

Palming is an easy exercise you can do to reduce the stress around your eyes. By placing your palms around your eyes and applying gentle pressure, you stimulate very powerful acupuncture points that help calm the mind, relax the muscles around the eyes, and bring healing energy to the eyes through increased circulation.

1. If you wear glasses or contact lenses, you should remove them.

2. Find a flat table or surface to sit at. Place your elbows on the table and lean forward comfortably.

3. Close your eyes gently. Now, place the palm of your left hand over your left eye, with your fingers touching your forehead. The hollow of your palm should be directly over the eye, but not touching it, leaving you room to blink. Rest the heel of your hand on your cheekbone.

4. Next, place your right hand over your right eye. As with the left, the hollow part of your palm should be over your eye with the heel of your hand resting on your cheekbone (see diagram above).

5. Make sure your elbows are low enough on the table so that your face and the weight of your head rest in your palms without placing any strain on your neck.

6. Remember to breathe while you do this exercise. Take several deep breaths to relax your body and calm your nervous system.

Palming gives you the opportunity to take a break from the ordinary work of seeing and allows you to simply relax your mind and eyes simultaneously. Even though palming should be done for only three minutes at a time, use this exercise as frequently as you like throughout the day to relax your eyes and soothe away the tensions of daily life.

~Marc Grossman, O.D., L.Ac.

www.visionworksusa.com

Magic Eye Viewing Techniques

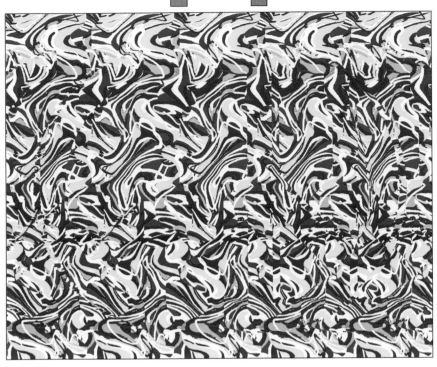

To view this image, refer to the instructions for diverging your eyes.

There are two methods for viewing Magic Eye images: diverging your eyes (focusing beyond the image) and converging your eyes (focusing before the image or crossing your eyes). Most of the Magic Eye images in this book have been created to be viewed by diverging your eyes. The back watermark of this book and the images on pages 9, 13, and 15 contain 3D images created to be viewed by converging your eyes.

Instructions #1 for Diverging Your Eyes (focusing beyond the image)

To reveal the hidden 3D illusion, hold the center of the image *right up to your nose*. It should be blurry. Focus as though you are looking *through* the image into the distance. *Very slowly* move the image away from your face until the two squares above the image turn into three squares. If you see four squares, move the image farther away from your face until you see three squares. If you see one or two squares, start over!

When you *clearly see three squares,* hold the page still, and the hidden image will slowly appear. Once you perceive the hidden image and depth, you can look around the entire 3D image. The longer you look, the clearer it becomes. The farther away you hold the page, the deeper it becomes.

Instructions #2 for Diverging Your Eyes (focusing beyond the image)

To reveal the hidden 3D illusion, hold the center of this image *right up to your nose*. It should be blurry. Focus as though you are looking *through* the image into the distance. *Very slowly* move the image away from your face until you begin to perceive depth. Now hold the page still and the hidden image will slowly appear.

Instructions for Converging Your Eyes (focusing before the image)

To reveal the hidden 3D illusion, hold the image at a comfortable reading distance, approximately 14 to 16 inches in front of your face. *Very slightly* cross your eyes until the two squares above the image turn into three squares. If you see four squares, cross your eyes even less until you see three squares. If you have a problem crossing your eyes, hold a pencil about halfway between you and the image. focus your eyes on the pencil tip while still being aware of the page. Keep trying until you see three squares on the page. When you *clearly see three squares,* hold the page still and the hidden image will slowly appear. Once you perceive the hidden image and depth, you can look around the entire 3D image. The longer you look, the clearer it becomes. The farther away you hold the page, the deeper it becomes.

Magic Eye "Floaters"

Magic Eye "floaters" are another type of Magic Eye 3D illusion. "Floaters" can first be viewed in 2D, then, by using the standard Magic Eye viewing techniques, "floaters" will appear to float in 3D space. (See pages 11 and 17.) Floaters and Magic Eye hidden illusions may be combined. (See page 33.)

Additional Viewing Information

Discipline is needed when a Magic Eye 3D illusion starts to "come in" because at that moment you will instinctively try to look at the page rather than looking through it, or before it. If you "lose it," start again.

If you converge your eyes and view an image created for diverging your eyes, the depth information comes out backward, and vice versa! This means if we intend to show an airplane flying in front of a cloud, if you converge your eyes you will see an airplane-shaped hole cut into the cloud! Another common occurrence is to diverge or converge your eyes twice as far as is needed to see the hidden image, as, for example, when you see four squares above the image instead of three. In this case, you will see a scrambled version of the intended object.

How Magic Eye May Improve Your Vision

In the United States, as in other highly technological countries, the ability to see clearly without glasses, contacts, or laser surgery has become the exception, not the rule. More than 100 million people in the United States are myopic (nearsighted). To put this figure into perspective, consider that the total U.S. population is just under 300 million, which means that approximately one out of every three people in this country experiences nearsightedness. When you look at it that way, you can see that we're facing a serious epidemic of myopia.

Why are so many people becoming nearsighted? Since less than 5 percent of Americans are born nearsighted, we can't blame our nation's nearsightedness just on our parents' genes. After nearly 25 years of practicing optometry, I've come to believe that the staggering number of Americans with myopia has more to do with how we live and the way we use our eyes than it does with genetics. For instance, it can't be simple coincidence that the years of onset correspond with the years of school, book learning, and computer work.

Most people become myopic during their first 18 years of life. The prevalence of nearsightedness increases with age: At 10 years of age, only 10 percent of the population is nearsighted; by age 15, the numbers rise to 25 percent and by age 18, 40 percent of Americans need corrective lenses for myopia. The statistics are even higher for students, with 60 percent of college students and 75 percent of graduate school students having myopia.

Biologically, the eyes simply are unsuited for the kinds of visual demands we place on them today. Because our ancestors were hunters and warriors who needed good vision in order to survive, the eyes evolved for clear, three-dimensional, fast-moving, and multifocused viewing, especially for seeing distance.

Myopia is a prime example of how function affects structure. With the advent of technology and the shift to a more literate culture, our lives today look quite different from those of our ancestors. Our culture has changed so quickly, our eyes haven't had time to adapt. The more time we spend absorbed in tasks that involve near vision, like reading or working on computers, the more difficult it becomes to see distance. Doing too many near-vision tasks for too long a time can frequently cause the ciliary muscles to contract. These muscles are responsible for seeing things close up, and if they are tightened for too long, it becomes more difficult for them to relax when our visual task is complete. Many research studies have shown that excessive near work can produce a nearsighted eye.

To understand how myopia develops, let's take a look at what vision really is. The function of the human eye is to create an image in your mind. But to understand how this works we must first understand the difference between sight and vision.

Sight is a physical occurrence that includes the retina, the eyeball, the lens, and the other physical parts of the eye. It involves acuity, the clarity of the image seen. On the level of pure sight, comprehension of the image is not important. In other words, we don't need to understand what we are seeing; we only need to see it clearly.

On the other hand, vision takes place within the mind as well as within our physical bodies. Vision involves more than the physical act of clearly seeing an image; it also entails our ability to understand the image that we've seen and then apply this information in a variety of ways. Comprehension, therefore, may be the key to our sense of vision. The greater our ability to comprehend, interpret, and use what we take in visually, the greater our sense of vision will be.

When you look at Magic Eye images, the brain merges one image from the right eye and one from the left eye into one three-dimensional image called *stereopsis,* which comes from the Greek word for "solid sight." Stereopsis is the appearance of depth when both eyes are used.

There is a strong association between the muscles that control the convergence angle of your eyes and the muscles that adjust the shape of the lens of the eye that focuses the image on your retina. These two sets of muscles usually work together. To see the Magic Eye images, however, the muscles must be coordinated somewhat separately, which benefits the visual system by keeping the eye muscles more flexible, adaptable, and relaxed. The Magic Eye images can also relax the mind and strengthen the eye-mind connection, allowing us to optimize our visual potential.

Instructions

To help improve your myopia, try this exercise. Remove your glasses and find a three-dimensional object in the distance to focus on that's somewhat blurry. Next, look at the Magic Eye images on the following pages. After you've looked at the images for about ten minutes, return your gaze to the same three-dimensional object you had looked at before. Does it appear clearer than it did before?

"I use the Magic Eye materials in my Vision Improvement Program, and they are very effective tools for teaching my patients better depth perception and effortless coordination."

~Samuel Berne, O.D.,
author of *Creating Your Personal Vision*

FFFFFFF

OOOOOOO

CCCCCC

UUUUUU

S S S S S S

3D Eye Chart

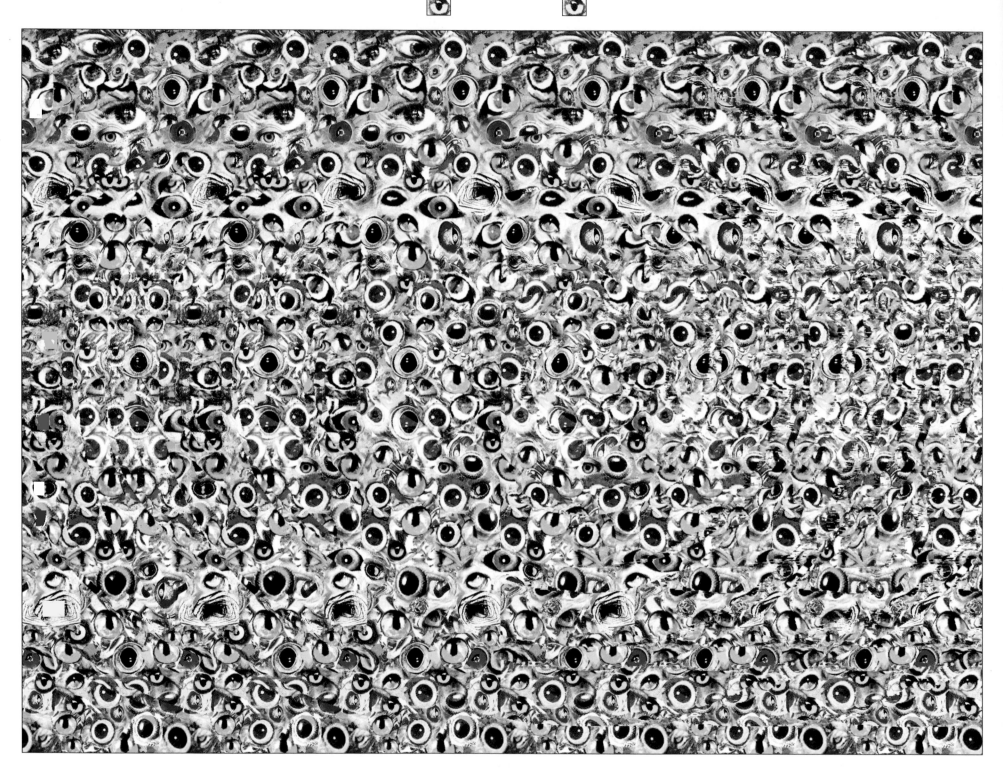

Follow the Spiral

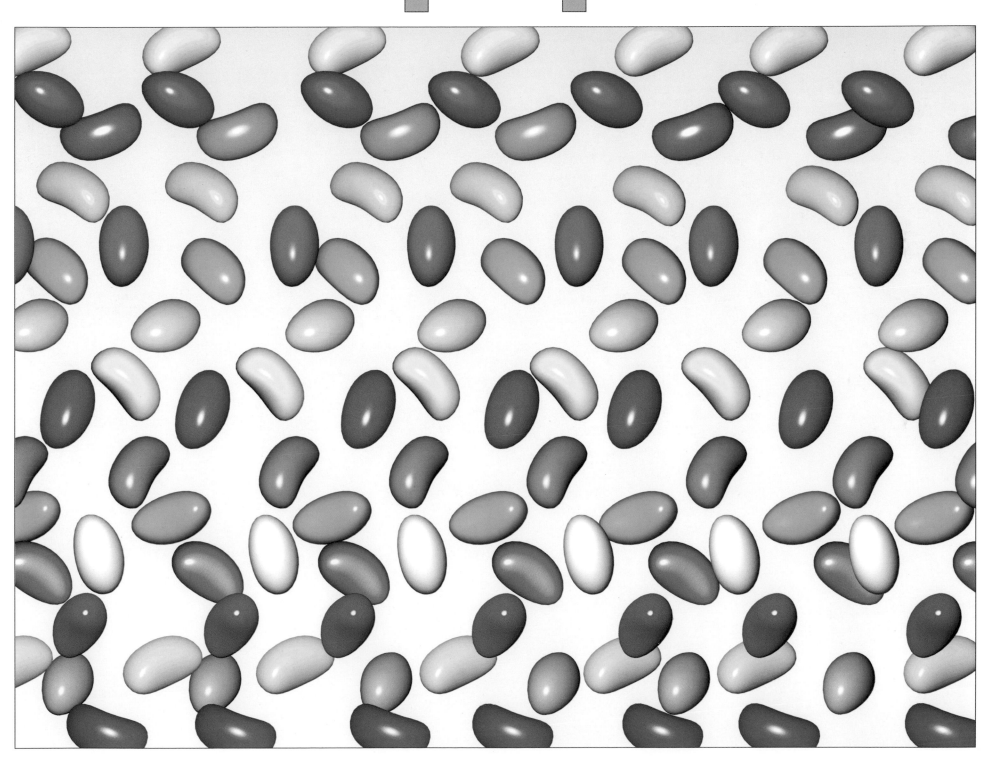

Jelly Beans

Magic Eye & Visual Skills

Maybe you have 20/20 eyesight, the visual prowess of Superman, able to leap tall buildings in a single bound or at least see far distances with clarity. Ready to flex your 3D visual muscles, you pick up a Magic Eye book only to discover your eyes aren't as picture perfect as you had thought.

The Magic Eye images aren't playing a game of hide and seek with you. To see the images, your eyes must work together as a coordinated team (binocular vision). Even if you have "perfect" distance vision, you may be one of the 20 million people in the United States affected by the common eye problem of binocular vision (eye teaming) difficulty.

The images in this section are designed to help with the visual skill of converging (turning your eyes in toward a target by slightly crossing your eyes) and diverging (turning your eyes out by focusing beyond the surface of the image). When binocular vision doesn't function properly, the eyes either can't align themselves or are unable to sustain alignment. Without ever knowing it, many people have one eye that "shuts down," mainly because the brain interprets the information it's receiving as conflicting, and your other eye takes over. The result is often blurry close-up vision or occasional double vision that many people write off as tired eyes.

Magic Eye images are a fun way to improve your visual skills. A 26-year-old accountant complained to me that he was able to see well in the morning but after eight hours of work, he experienced eye strain, discomfort, and blurred vision. Ten minutes of Magic Eye exercises twice a day, along with regular breaks to relax his eyes, enhanced his eye coordination and focusing skills to the point that his eyes work more comfortably and efficiently together and his eye strain is gone.

Now it's time to go to the "eye gym." The following images will help with eye focusing and coordination. As you view in 3D, breathe deeply and blink; the image and the depth will continue to increase. Move your attention gradually around the page. To make the exercise more challenging, vary the distance between yourself and the page. Move the page farther and then closer to your eyes. Close and then open your eyes. Does the image come right back, or is it gone? If it disappeared, notice what your eyes and mind have to do in order to bring it back.

After five minutes of converging and diverging Magic Eye images, give your eyes a rest and do the palming exercise (instructions on page 6) before trying another 3D exercise.

Congratulations! You've just made it through a Magic Eye workout.

"I work as a vision therapist. Magic Eye pictures are a fun way to get kids to learn to diverge their eyes."

~Charlotte Phillips, Wichita, Kansas

"In the past year I have learned to view Magic Eye images and I've found that my vision has improved. I used to have to wear glasses to drive but now I don't."

~Lisa Ezzell, Lakeland, Florida

"I have been a fan of Magic Eye since the first product came out. My daughter has a lazy eye and has been helped tremendously by these exercises. The images work on the same level as the expensive 3D exercises performed at her doctor's office. Thank you for providing a product that is both fun and useful."

~Patricia Leonard, Farner, Tennessee

"I visited my eye doctor; he said that rather than put prisms in my glasses, to use Magic Eye cards daily for six months! It seems to work. I used them faithfully for a number of years and then I got lazy and didn't use them for six months. My vision deteriorated to the point of needing prisms after that. I am starting to use Magic Eye for eye exercises again."

~Linda Ahern, Springfield, Oregon

"When I was about nine, I got so frustrated because I nearly needed glasses. Just by learning to see Magic Eye, I managed to adjust my focus and ended up with 20/20 vision. I'm glad as I now have braces too. Aahhhhhhh!"

~Hannah B., Essex, England

"I was unable to see the images hidden in the depths of the brilliantly colored prints on the wall of an optometrist's office. Then, one day, the doctor told me to try it without my glasses and I was hooked! For the first time since I was in the fifth grade, I could see something clearly without my glasses! Magic Eye has a reader for life in me."

~Norma Popp, Batavia, Ohio

View this Magic Eye 3D image by diverging your eyes.

Instructions #1 for Converging Your Eyes (focusing before the image)

To reveal the hidden 3D illusion, hold the image at a comfortable reading distance directly in front of your face. *Very slightly* cross your eyes until the two squares above the image turn into three squares. If you see four squares, cross your eyes even less until you see three squares. When you *clearly see three squares*, hold the page still, and the hidden image will slowly appear. Once you perceive the hidden image and depth, you can look around the entire 3D image. The longer you look, the clearer it becomes. The farther away you hold the page, the deeper it becomes. After you correctly converge your eyes to view this Magic Eye 3D image, notice how the 3D illusion appears to float in midair in front of the page. Try to reach out and touch the illusion with your hand.

Instructions #2 for Converging Your Eyes (focusing before the image)

Hold a pencil or your finger about halfway between you and the image. Focus your eyes on the pencil or finger tip while still being aware of the page. Keep trying until you see three squares on the page. When you *clearly see three squares* hold the page still and the hidden image will slowly appear.

Instructions for Diverging Your Eyes (focusing beyond the image)

To reveal the hidden 3D illusion, hold the center of the image right up to your nose. It should be blurry. Focus as though you are looking *through* the image. *Very slowly* move the image away from your face until the two squares above the image turn into three squares. If you see four squares, move the image farther away from your face until you see three squares. If you see one or two squares, start over!

When you *clearly have three squares* hold the page still, and the hidden image will slowly appear. Once you perceive the hidden image and depth, you can look around the entire 3D image. The longer you look, the clearer it becomes. The further away you hold the page, the deeper it becomes.

After you correctly diverge your eyes to view this Magic Eye 3D image, notice how the page appears to be a "window" you "look into" to view the 3D illusion. The 3D Illusion is contained "inside" or "within" the page.

Magic Eye "Floaters"

Once you are "locked into" the depth of this 3D image, take notice of the row of 3D dolphins along the bottom of the image. They will appear to float in 3D space. We call this illusion Magic Eye 3D "floaters."

View this Magic Eye 3D image by converging your eyes.

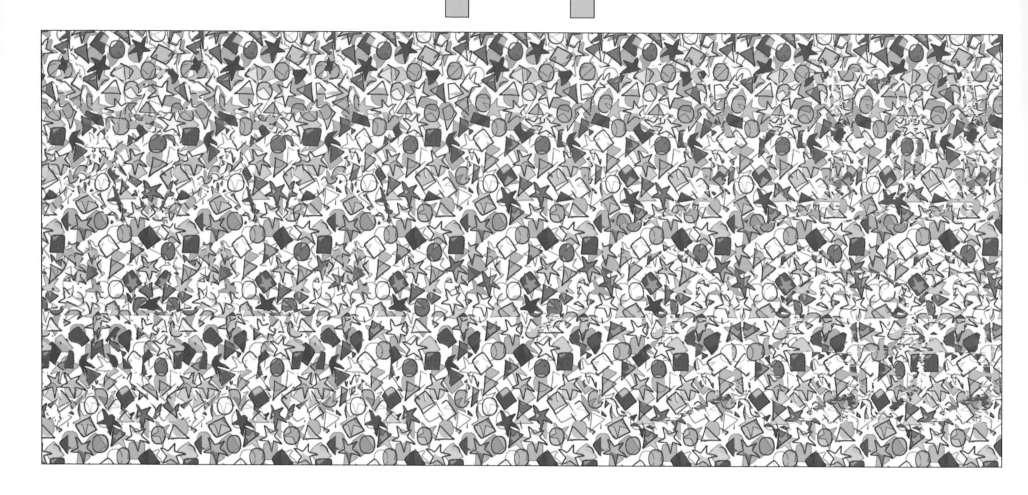

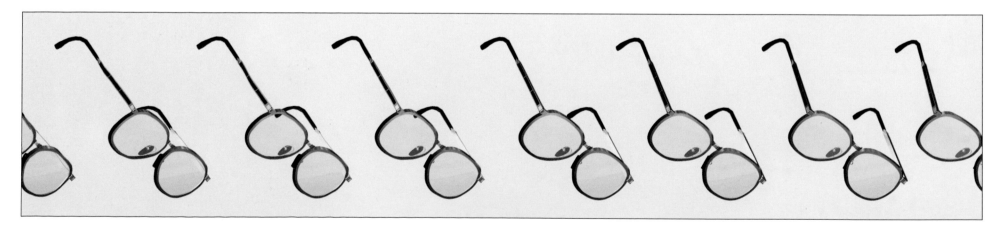

View this Magic Eye 3D image by diverging your eyes.

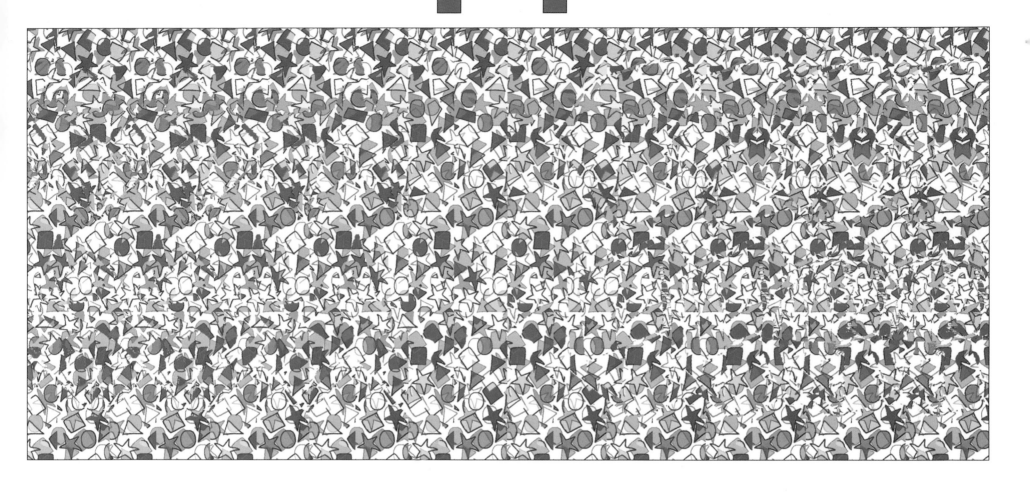

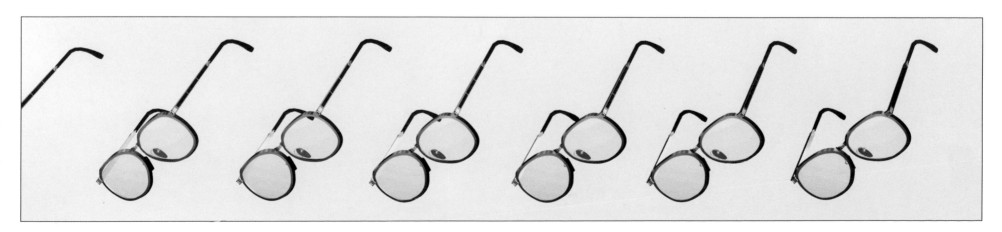

View this Magic Eye 3D image by converging your eyes.

Magic Eye & Computer Eye Strain

It's hard to imagine life without computers. Over one-third of the American population uses computers on a regular basis. And more than half complain of eye strain, headaches, blurred vision, and other visual symptoms related to sustained computer work. It's easy to get absorbed in our work, or surfing the Net, or even playing a game. Before we know it, hours may have gone by without our looking up from the screen. To stay healthy and functioning their best, our eyes need to look at a variety of distances, as well as relax. The prolonged stress of close vision taxes the visual system and can lead to other problems, too, like body fatigue and reduced efficiency at work.

If you experience any of these symptoms, you can relieve eye strain through a combination of different approaches, like correcting your workstation conditions, adjusting your posture, using stress-relieving lenses prescribed specifically for computer operation, adding a special antiglare screen to your computer, and practicing Magic Eye exercises.

Just as your hamstrings can get sore from a long run, the muscles in your eyes can become strained from overuse. When we do a near-vision task for a prolonged period of time—like working on the computer—we put enormous demand on specific eye muscles, namely the ciliary muscle that controls the lens of the eye and the extraocular muscles that control the ability to converge our eyes onto a target. Over time, these muscles simply get tired or accustomed to being in one position.

How can Magic Eye images help relieve computer-induced eye strain? Viewing the hidden 3D images requires the eye muscles to work in the opposite direction, giving them a chance to rebalance. Seeing the image also depends on the eyes working together more efficiently as a team, which requires them to learn how to look in a more relaxed manner. Over time, Magic Eye exercises can help the flexibility of these overworked eye muscles and alleviate much of the eye strain you experience while working on the computer.

"To keep my eyes healthy while spending long hours on computers, I take periodic 'vision breaks' to refocus and relax my eyes; viewing Magic Eye images helps, specifically exercising divergence."

~David A. Sheppard,
computer consultant

"I have your books and have been using them for about a year as a type of 'therapy.' 3D viewing relaxes my eyes after reading or concentrating at a computer, and my mind becomes clearer and more focused."

~Michael Gest, Boulder, Colorado

"After I work at a computer screen all day, Magic Eye is a great exercise for my eyes. I would like to be adult and say that I look at them for purely medical reasons but I can't. Magic Eye is just plain fun."

~Lori S. Snow, Hilliard, Ohio

"I work for a telecom company and I produce many reports, which need to be closely scrutinized. I have to analyze the data for the reports, and proofread the end results before publishing the reports. I get eye strain from looking at the screen too much. Every now and then I'll go to magiceye.com to 'exercise' my eyeballs. I feel a bit of instant relief when I look at the images. Plus it's fun!"

~Lisa K. Bennett, Cedar Rapids, Iowa

"What else is there to say? Magic Eye must be one of the best ways to exercise your eyes and have fun at the same time! It's a fantastic discovery and should be introduced into the school curriculum."

~Derek Mackay, Aberdeenshire, Scotland

"I work at a computer all day and find looking at a Magic Eye picture now and then provides much-needed relief from eye strain. And, they're fun!"

~Helen, Woldoboro, Maine

"It wasn't fun to know that everyone was seeing the hidden picture, until I discovered the joy myself. Now my eyes are stuck in only one place; what fun."

~Hendrik Edwin, Bloemfontein, South Africa

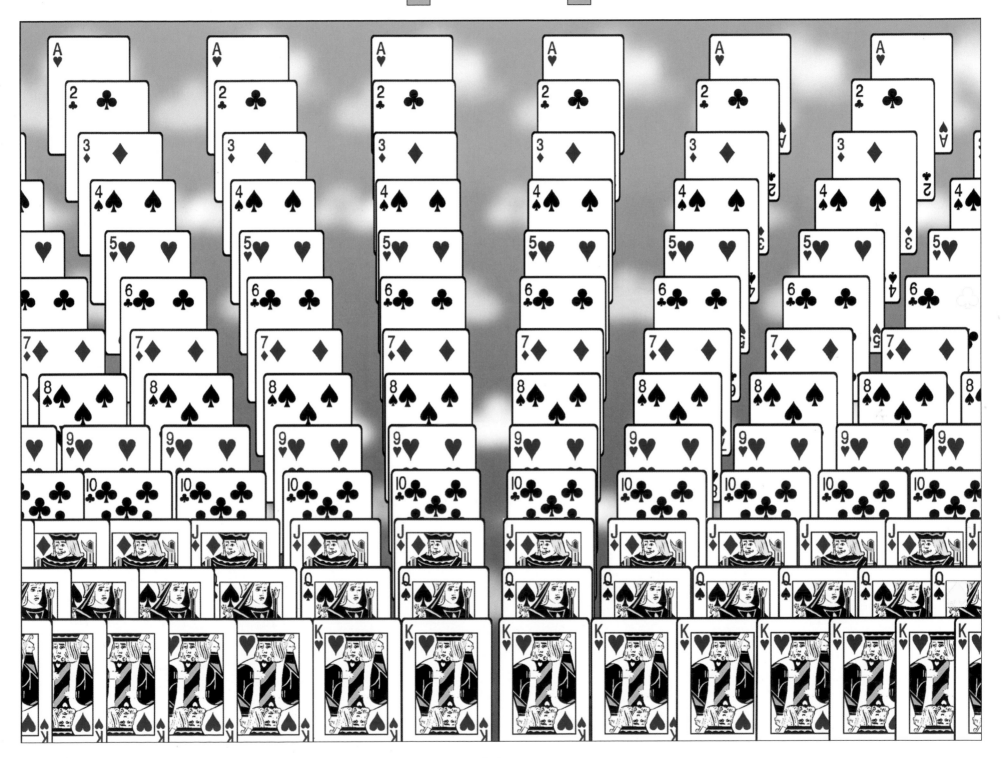

Solitaire

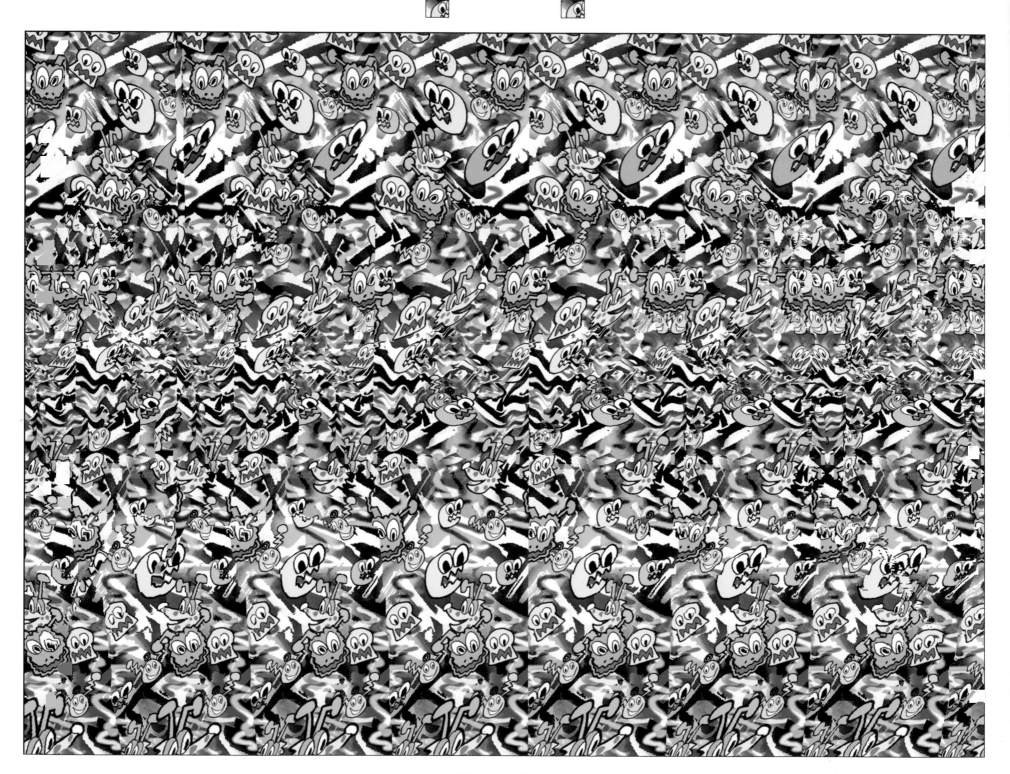

Computer Bugs

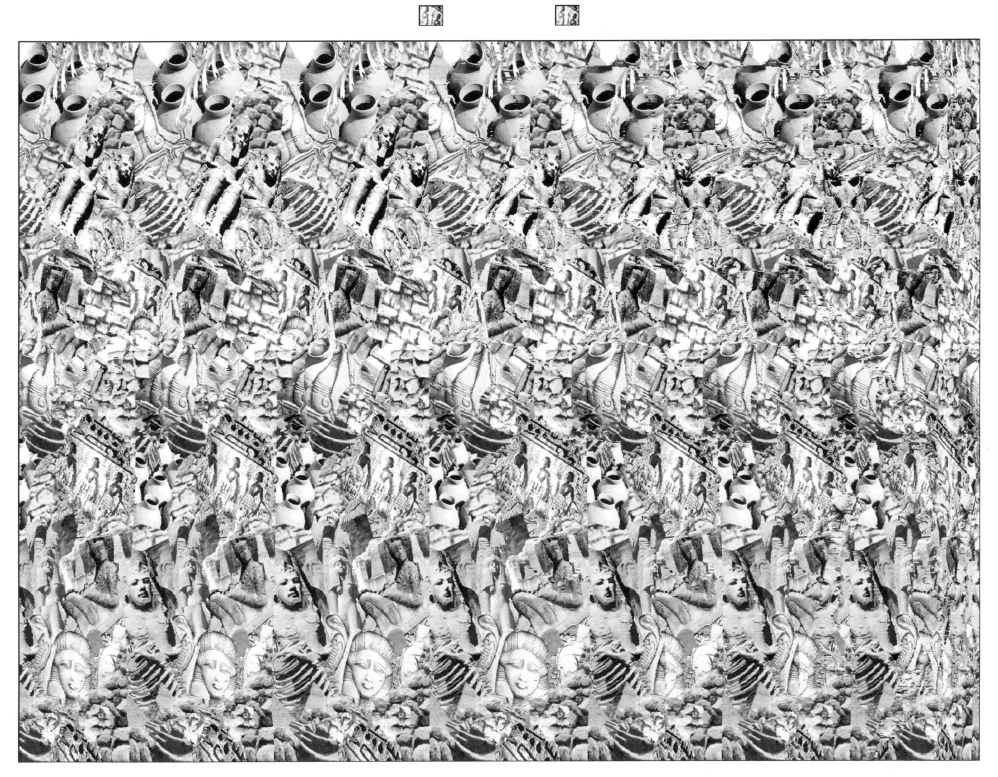

A Closer View

Magic Eye, Accelerated Learning & Fast Reading

*T*he endless piles on your desk. The bottomless pit of e-mail in your inbox. Professional magazines stacked by your bed. The morning newspaper. The amount of print information we have to sort through every day is utterly overwhelming.

What if you could use Magic Eye images to turbocharge your reading? What if you could absorb information into and beyond the range of 25,000 words a minute?

A private school in Minnesota, Learning Strategies Corporation, has developed an exciting learning technology to increase reading speed and improve comprehension. With the PhotoReading Whole Mind System you can use Magic Eye images to develop the skills to blast through books as fast as you can turn the pages.

Magic Eye images help you enter a state of relaxed alertness, making it easier to access expanded capabilities of mind such as "mentally photographing" the printed page. When you view Magic Eye images, your eyes learn a soft focus that feeds visual information directly into the other-than-conscious (subconscious) mind. On the other hand, hard focus—our normal way of looking at printed material—sends discrete pieces of information through the conscious mind. By using this soft focus, instead of slowly identifying individual words or word groups, you achieve the soft gaze to notice the entire page at once. So put on your seat belts, take a deep breath, and view the following Magic Eye images to tap into your limitless potential to learn.

"The gaze used when viewing a Magic Eye image produces the same effect we want when PhotoReading. For years we described it as 'seeing with soft eyes' and have shown references back to ancient China, Korea, and Japan. Using it when walking in the world gives us the ability of seeing into the essence of things, instead of getting stuck observing the surface appearance and external movement of our environment. Using this gaze, we bypass the critical faculty of the conscious mind and connect to more vastly capable regions of our brain through pathways we rarely use in our daily lives. Who would have imagined that viewing Magic Eye images would give you access to such power? You can use it to read faster and live more fully!"

~Paul R. Scheele, Chairman,
Learning Strategies Corporation;
author of *PhotoReading* and *Natural Brilliance*

"I have seen Paul Scheele help countless numbers of people to discover a faster, more efficient path to success through his PhotoReading system. No matter what you need to read, he can teach you to get it done in a third of the time."

~Anthony Robbins,
author of *Awaken the Giant Within*
and *Unlimited Power*

"Magic Eye is brilliantly relaxing and apparently a very useful eye exercise when training for PhotoReading! Love to discover the hidden images."

~Ute Hirsekorn, Nottingham, United Kingdom

"Magic Eye seems to connect me with a part of my mind I didn't know existed"

~Amy Sands, San Francisco, California

"After learning to view Magic Eye pictures, I tried looking at the 'real' world as if it were a Magic Eye picture. I am noticing so many things I overlooked before."

~Toni Black, Austin, Texas

"I love Magic Eye. I think it helps me to concentrate. When I can't focus, I look at my Magic Eye book and then I seem to be able to focus on other things better."

~Mark Garnier, Toronto, Canada

"Magic of magic Eye magically improved my vision and concentration. I always view the pictures to improve further."

~Mangesh Kulkarni, Pune, India

"This may sound weird, I know you look at Magic Eye pictures with your eyes, but I think looking at the pictures expanded my mind."

~Dale Roberts, Australia

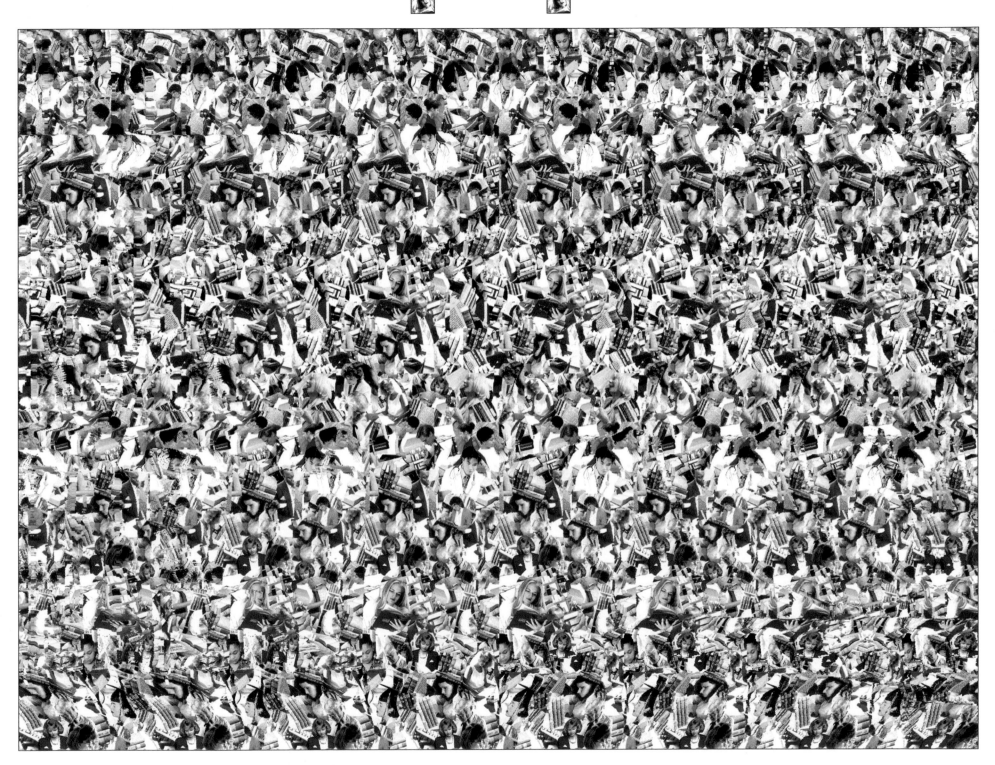

Limitless Potential

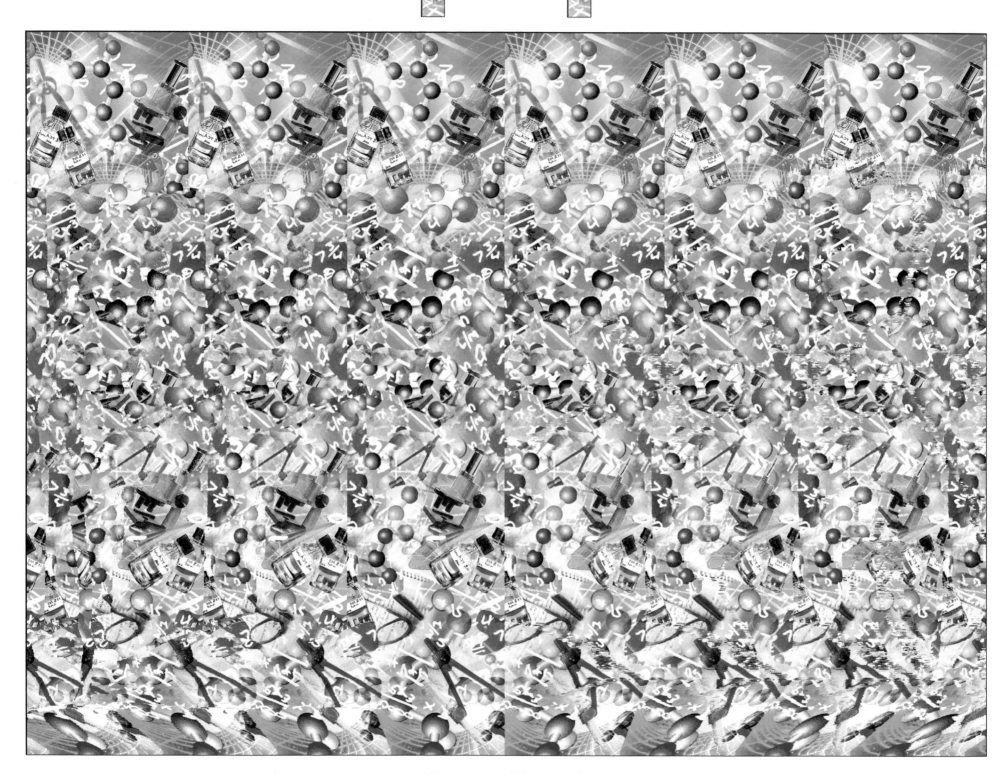

Discover the Unexpected

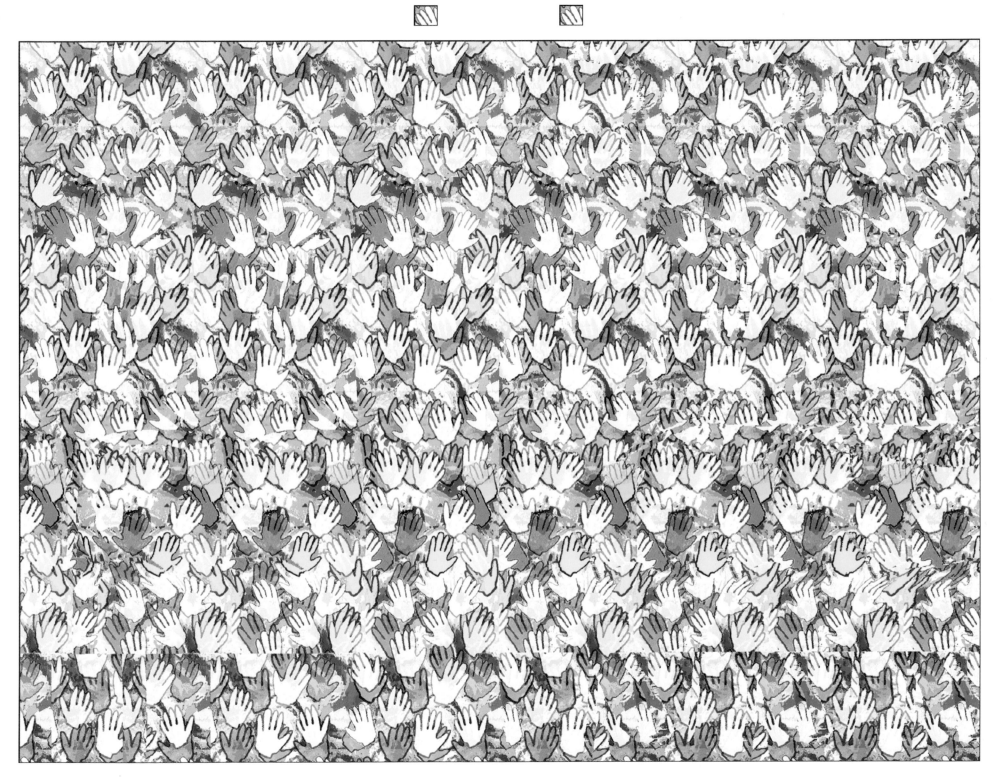

Helping Hands

Magic Eye & Sports

Do you wish you could improve your batting average in the weekend softball league? Cut a few strokes off your golf score? Take your tennis game to the next level? Did you know that vision is just as important as speed or strength in how well you play a sport?

Coordination, concentration, balance, and accuracy are just a few of the visually related skills you use during a sports event. Vision affects your batting average, racquetball score, pass completion, and free throw percentages.

When you train for a sport, you might work on your aerobic capacity, endurance, strength, muscle tone, or flexibility. But coaches, trainers, and eye doctors now say you should train your vision as well. The stamina, flexibility, and fine-tuning of your visual system can sometimes provide that split-second timing you need to truly excel at your chosen sport. In many sports, one of the most important visual skills is the ability to have stereopsis (depth perception). Many studies show that professional athletes have much better visual skills than non-athletes, which helps them anticipate and respond more quickly to complex visual conditions. In particular, athletes often have greater stereopsis (depth perception) than the ordinary person.

In many sports, depth perception is one of the most crucial visual skills. It allows you to judge the distance and speed of objects. So the better your depth perception is, the more quickly and accurately you can see the baseball whooshing toward your bat.

Professional athletes and their coaches have found that vision contributes so significantly to sports performance that it may be the key factor that differentiates a good athlete from an exceptional one. For instance, studies reveal that major league players test higher on stereopsis than minor league players.

The Magic Eye images on the following pages will enhance your stereo vision to help you increase your depth perception. So the next time you play tennis, throw a football, or shoot hoops, you'll really be able to keep your eye on the ball.

"Magic Eye 3D pictures are great tools for exploring the 'soft focus' that can lead to performance breakthroughs."

~Nathaniel Zinsser, Ph.D,
member of the U.S. Olympic Committee's
Sport Psychology Registry

"Vision training including Magic Eye images has helped my visual concentration and depth judgments. It enhanced my performance in both tennis and in the martial arts."

~Michael Edson,
former tennis teacher and martial arts instructor

"In basketball my team needs me to 'see it all.' I use the same type of focus during games as I use to view Magic Eye pictures."

~Cory Speicher, Livingston, New Jersey

"I recommend Magic Eye pictures as a technique to help visual concentration and depth perception for my students."

~Ellen Marshall,
ice skating instructor

"Magic Eye is like weight training for my eyes."

~Dennis Ponte, San Jose, California

"In sports it's all about how much you can see. Viewing Magic Eye images is one of the simplest and most effective ways to learn to fully 'open up' your field of vision."

~Loren Quinby, Phoenicia, New York

"Any system for improving eye-hand coordination, depth perception, and peripheral vision would be a surefire method for improving athletic performance."

~Keith Meliones,
school psychologist and softball coach

"I love viewing Magic Eye pictures. They have helped me see better when I play soccer."

~Jessica Ente, age 12, Dix Hills, New York

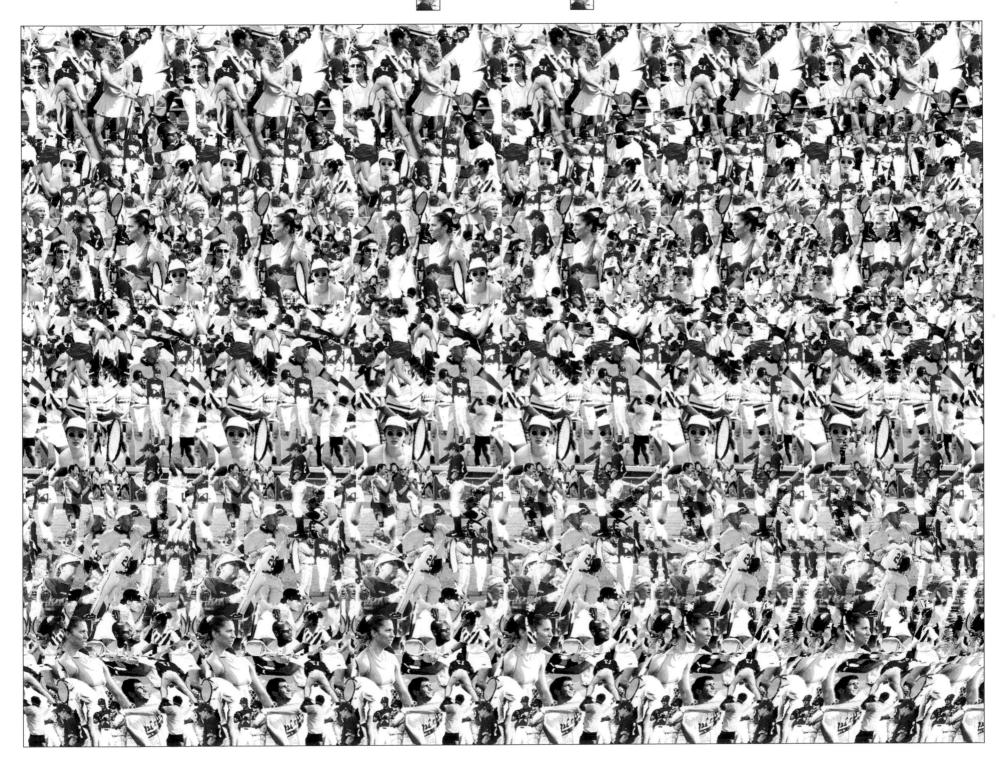

Swingers

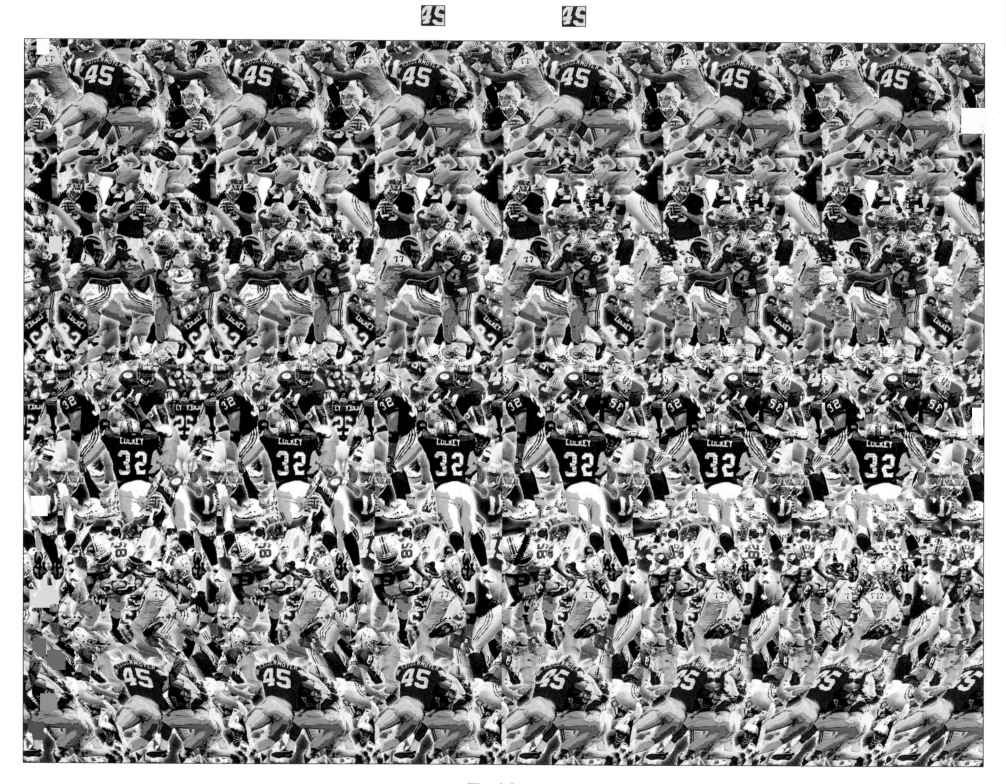

Touchdown

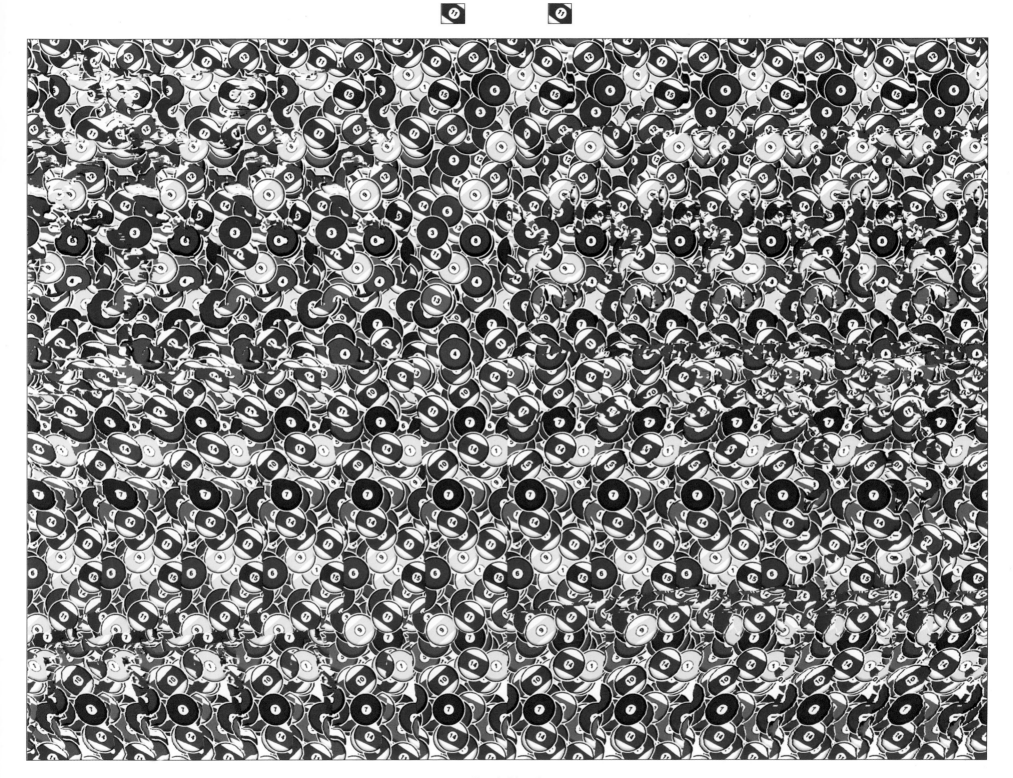

Pool Sharks

Magic Eye & the Brain

Your friends are all getting it. "Wow!" they're saying. "Look at this one—it's amazing!"

You let your mind relax and your vision soften as you go deeper and deeper into the image. Suddenly, almost by magic, a hidden picture begins to form. "I get it!" you shout, totally elated, grinning to yourself, happier and more connected to the world than you've felt in a while.

Can Magic Eye images really affect your mood and make you calmer or happier? It sounds like a big claim to make, but, in fact, studies have shown that these images can have a positive effect on relieving stress. Sure, the images are a lot of fun to look at. But did you know that viewing them may actually change your brain chemistry? That's because your eyes and your brain have to work as partners to establish the soft focus gaze you need to view the hidden images.

The human brain consists of billions of nerve cells. These cells exchange tiny electrochemical impulses among themselves and through the central nervous system. These electrochemical discharges create the signals we call brainwaves, which can be measured with an electroencephalogram, or EEG.

In preliminary experiments, researchers studied the brainwaves of people while they were looking at Magic Eye images. After the subjects saw the hidden images, the EEG recorded more alpha waves, which is a type of brain activity that occurs in relaxed states like meditation. In fact, the technique for viewing Magic Eye images is very similar to the meditation procedures described in many Eastern religions. Some people believe that increased alpha waves can make you feel calmer, more receptive, and more creative.

So, to make your brain happy, view the following Magic Eye pictures for ten minutes a day. Besides having fun, you could enter into a more alpha state of mind.

"Magic Eye pictures are a wonderful way to help people get in touch with how their brain works."

~Jay Lombard, D.O.,
director of the Brain Behavior Center,
Rockland County, New York

"The Magic Eye images shift perception and evoke predictable dominant brainwave signatures and awaken us to a new sense of enjoyable possibility through awareness."

~John L. Fritz,
mind/body researcher

"I am a teacher and I use Magic Eye to talk about vision and how our brain works. It's not just educational, it's fun and entertaining!"

~Rosemary T. Hornak, Ph.D., Raleigh, North Carolina

"The experience of looking at stereograms and merging them in my brain (to experience 3D) gave me an altered state of mind when the experience of space clicked in. With a sophisticated brainwave plotter, it was made clear that indeed an alpha brain wave state is induced naturally."

~Rudie Berkhout,
artist/holographer

"I love Magic Eye. I have ADHD, which makes concentrating kind of hard. Independently of my doctor, I found that using Magic Eye pictures helped my concentration skills. The doctor was quite impressed and has started recommending it to other people he treats!"

~David Roberts, Summerville, South Carolina

"Magic Eye is exciting, a fat-free form of instant gratification, every bit as satisfying as chocolate cake."

~Billie Gates, Alberta, Canada

"I LOVE Magic Eye. . . . It has changed the way I view LIFE!!!! Thank you for giving me such happiness!!!"

~Dana Madrid, LaMesa, California

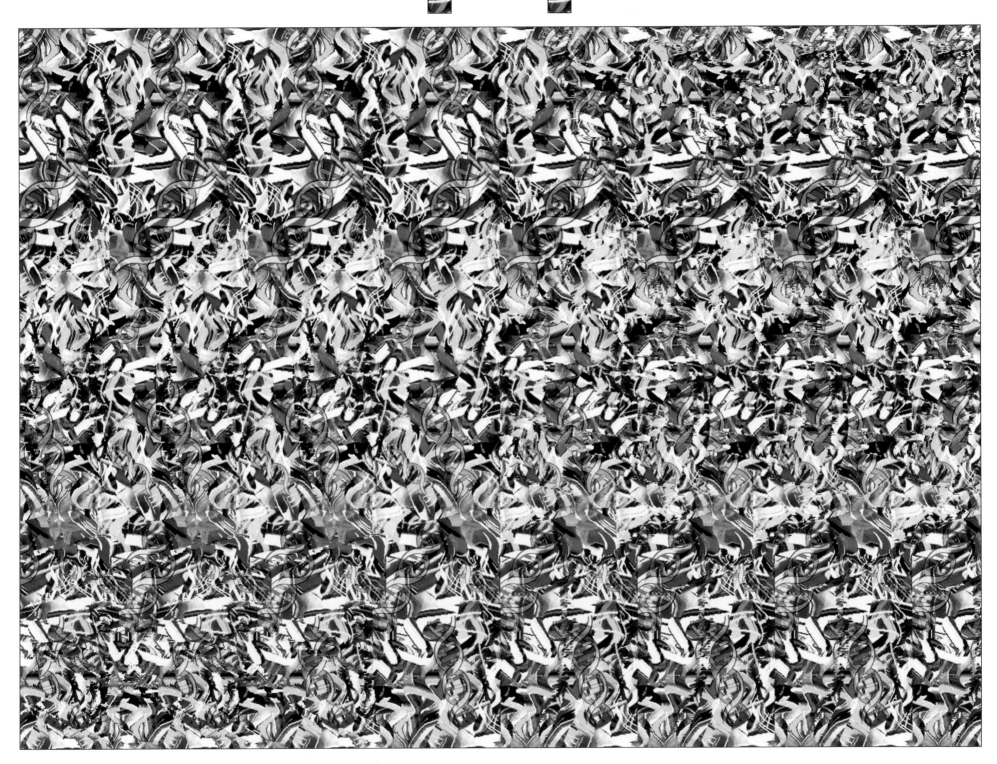

Double Helix

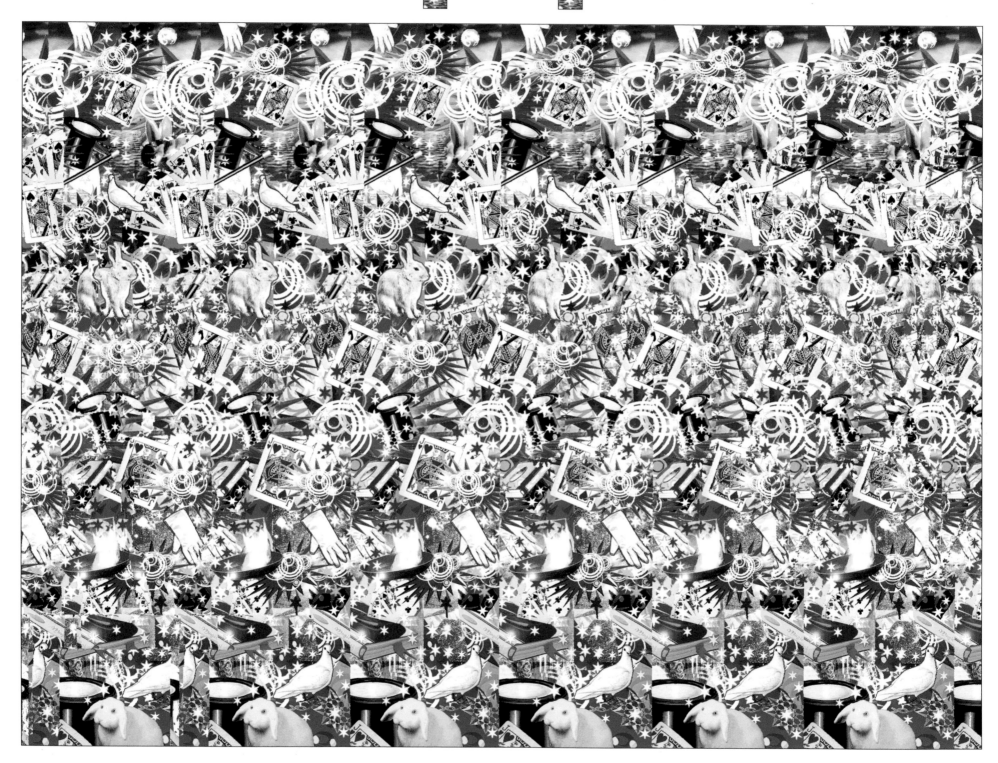

The Magician

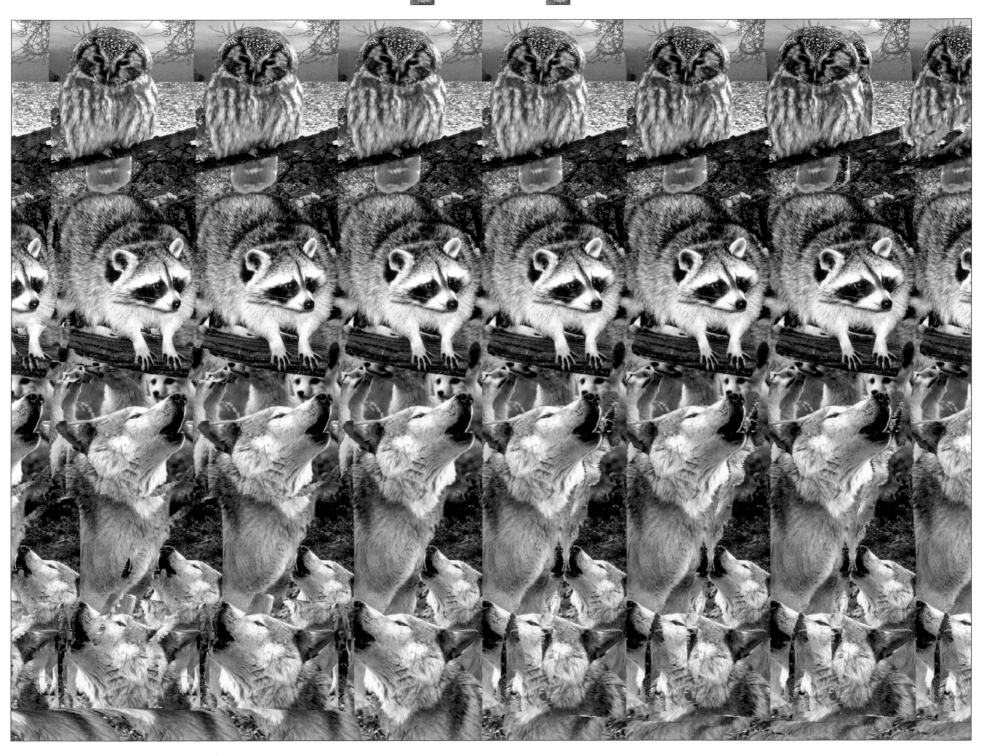

Call of the Wild

Magic Eye & Inner Peace

We have all had days when we feel out of balance, when nothing seems to go right. How's this for a likely scenario: a hard day at the office, followed by terrible traffic on the commute home, and when you do get home, the kids are unruly, a headache's tugging at your temples, and you just want to unwind. Just that morning you had a few moments of peace. Where did it go? How can you return to that calm balance?

That's right! It's time for Magic Eye.

Magic Eye helps develop the basic principle of mind-body unity. When people view the hidden picture in the Magic Eye image, they experience a moment of integration: physical, mental, and spiritual energies all flow together to create an enhanced sense of health and well-being.

If the mind is chronically restless or agitated, the health of the body will become compromised. By helping quiet the mind of distracting thoughts and taking in the visual image in a deep way, the practice of viewing Magic Eye images can help counter such ill effects.

Magic Eye images may affect the specialized neurotramsmitters that get released when you experience that feeling of "inner peace." It may work by increasing the production of the neurotransmitter serotonin, the neurotransmitter of "inner peace." Serotonin levels increase when we have that "aha" experience, the natural high of seeing the Magic Eye image.

Increased serotonin levels can affect our perceptions dramatically. All balanced emotional conditions, and even such elevated states as happiness and joy, are associated with normal or high serotonin levels. On the other hand, insecurity, anger, fear, depression, and other agitated emotional states are associated with low serotonin levels. When serotonin levels are high, we can experience a conscious state of thoughtful satisfaction. Just like when we "get" a Magic Eye hidden image.

> *"As you consciously relax and experience these Magic Eye 3D pictures, they can effortlessly help you cultivate a wondrous meditative state."*
>
> ~Sudhir Jonathan Foust,
> president, Kripalu Center for Yoga and Health

> *"I find myself drawn into Magic Eye and all the cares and stress of the world are lightened."*
>
> ~K. Treman, Sturgis, Michigan

> *"I love Magic Eye images so much. Both of my kids gave me separate posters for my birthday. To me, it's the coolest way to relax and pass time, just staring into space and watching a picture appear. It's stunning, it's amazing and a WONDER!"*
>
> ~Doris Lord, Hampton, Georgia

> *"Magic Eye is like the ninth wonder of the world. It has a sense of going into your own 'other dimension.' They are very interesting and fun. It's a hidden treasure."*
>
> ~Esther Gomez, Alvin, Texas

> *"Balancing the right and left side of the brain balances our inner male and female sides. This balanced state helps us to stay in present time, which in turn makes it easy to tune in to our own inner voice. Listening to our own inner voice allows us to make choices that are best for us, in our power, and keeps us out of confusion."*
>
> ~Sarah Smith, coordinator,
> Awakenings Clairvoyance School

> *"Magic Eye helps me forget about the pressures of life and lets me live in a dream world, if only for a few moments."*
>
> ~Chris McCamlie, Barnet, Herts, England

> *"I enjoy your art so much. I find it so relaxing and outstanding."*
>
> ~Aida Y. Peel, Panama City, Florida

> *"I am 50 years old. It was some time ago that I first was introduced to Magic Eye by a friend who was simply fascinated with it. I can actually recall the feeling of awe the first time I looked and this amazing 3D image came into view. I still have the same feeling today. I adore it!"*
>
> ~Barbara Ann Cavallaro, Philladelphia, Pennsylvania

> *"I have a very stressful job, but when I look at Magic Eye images, it literally takes away all the stress."*
>
> ~Connie Kathleen Baker, Flint, Michigan

Butterfly Promenade

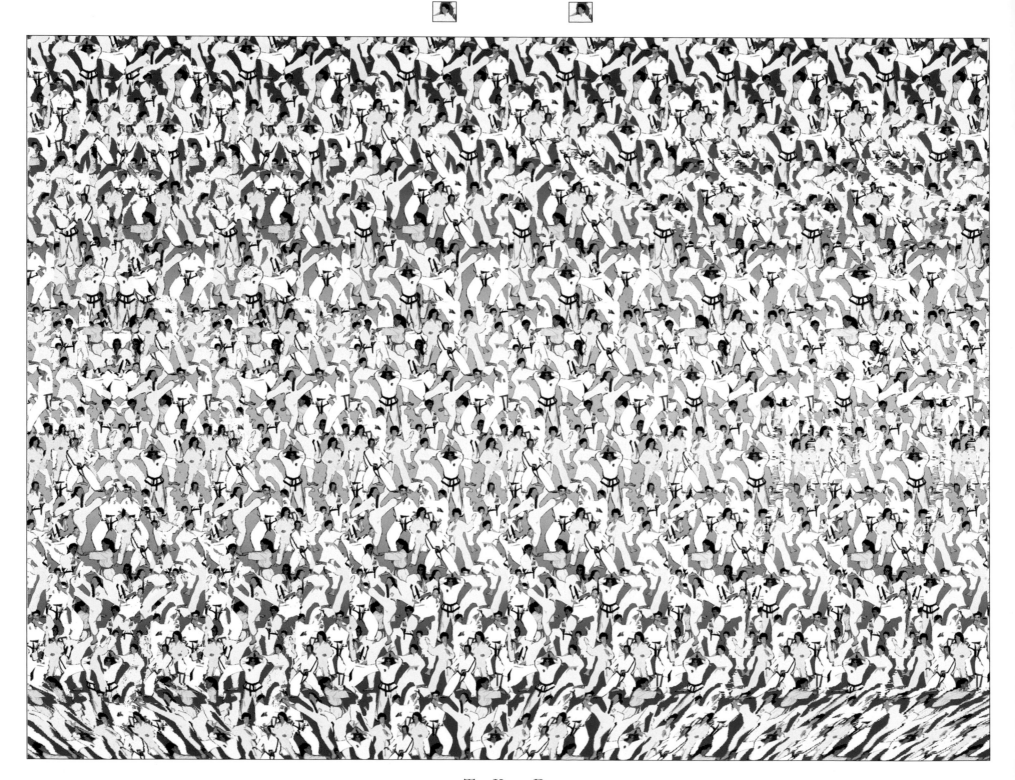

Tae Kwon Do

Under the Sea

Magic Eye & Intuition

Have you ever thought of someone you haven't spoken to in years and suddenly they call you? Or were you ever at the racetrack and had a certain "feeling" about a horse, though your logical mind says you'd be crazy to place the bet, and then the horse wins. Is it coincidence? Luck? Or the voice of your intuition saying, "Listen to me!"

Everyone possesses this intuitive ability. Yet most of us barely scratch the surface of our natural intuitive abilities. Intuition is the part of our consciousness that has knowledge without ever being directly taught. It is our consciousness's link with all of existence.

Even if you think you don't have an intuitive bone in your body, the good news is it's possible to develop this ability.

The key to intuition is presence. When you are truly present in the moment, you are not "thinking" about the past or future; your intellect is not engaged. This lack of engagement enables you to access your intuition. What does it mean to be present? You are present when you notice beauty, when you have a creative thought, when you stop to hear a child laughing. True presence is timeless, and can be accompanied by many feelings including wonder, heartfelt joy, laughter, peace, stillness, and "knowing."

Many people also experience presence while viewing Magic Eye images. While viewing the next two Magic Eye images, try to notice how presence feels to you. Notice your thoughts, how your mind seems to stop its usual chatter while you are looking at the images. Try to stay present for the entire time you are looking into the Magic Eye images. Begin by looking at each image for a minimum of one minute.

Following are instructions for an intuitive exercise using the Magic Eye labyrinth image on page 39.

Once you see the hidden image, let your eyes slowly follow the path between the raised lines through the labyrinth. Begin from the outside until you reach the center of the image. As you journey along the path feel your body drifting into a meditative state. When you reach the center, rest your eyes here for a moment. Take notice of how you feel, and what thoughts arise. Something may happen, and something may not. This is an exercise of presence. The more you practice this state of being in present time, the more your intuition will develop.

Feel how refreshed your mind and body can be with this simple exercise.

"I have found that the Magic Eye experience appears to enhance your ability to see the unseen and to feel the unmanifest components of nature. It is an excellent aide to exercise your psychic ability."

~Dr. Catherine Sweet, D.C.

"Our vision is so important. As we learn to look past the surface and see what is behind that which is presented to us, our intuition takes over and we are able to really 'see' what is going on. It is then that we are reading the energy of a situation or a certain person. This is the gift of sight that we all hold, but sometimes need to take the time to develop it to its full potential."

~Sharon Turner, founder and teacher, Awakenings Clairvoyance School

"In that 'aha' moment when a Magic Eye image pops out at you—you are not in your thinking mind, you are in the 'now.' The left and right brain—the left and right eyes—are working together. They are in a state of coherence. You are ready to accept some 'thing' unknown. (The hidden image.) In that coherence and acceptance, the present moment opens up. Thinking stops and you become the 'Beholder,' the 'See-er,' that is so much more 'You' than your thinking mind."

~Lynn McKenna, songwriter

"I have many Magic Eye books. I love them and I practice with them regularly, because I think they are a marvelous tool for spiritual advancement. Opening the third eye and developing second sight, seeing beyond the normal field of vision, seeing auras and so forth. Excellent! Thank you so much. Learning to see 'through' your pictures over the years has truly enhanced my life!"

~Mandi Johnson, West Yorkshire, England

"Besides being a portal into a new dimension of our world, it is great exercise for the eyes! I love it!"

~Nicholas H. Bomba, Glenville, New York

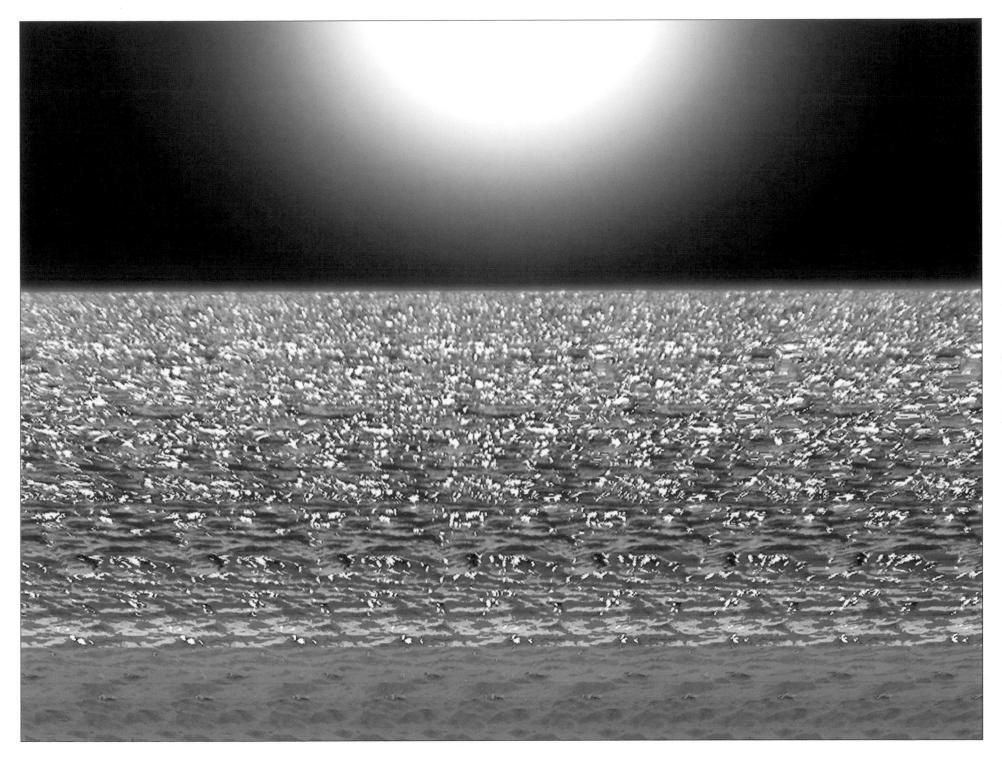

Tranquility

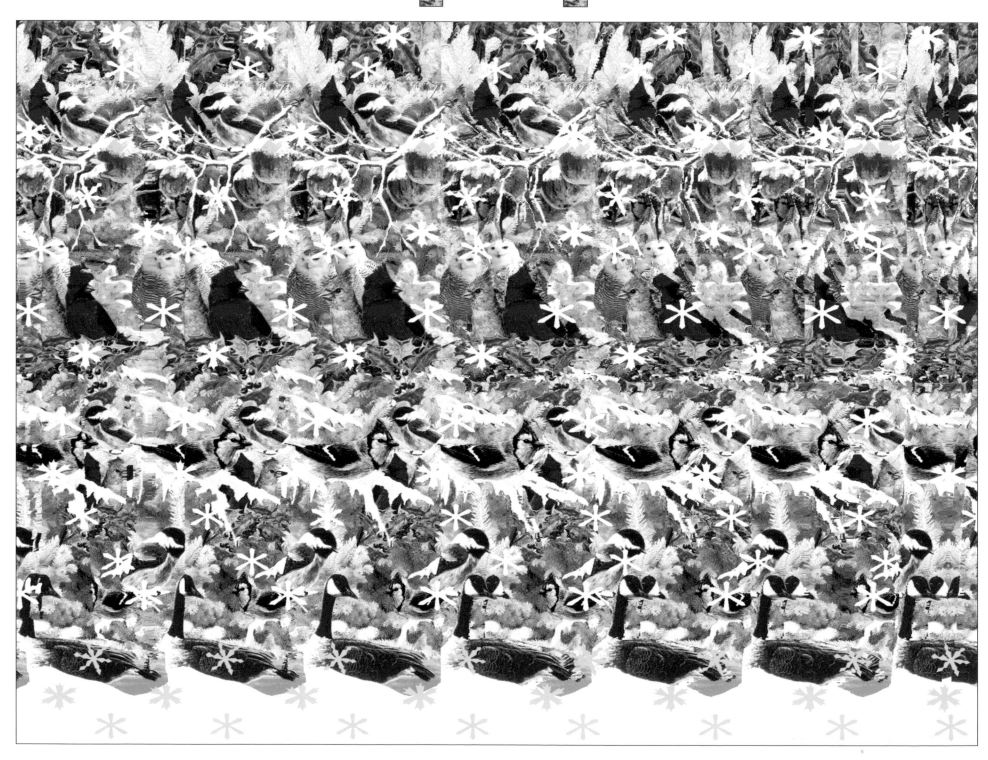

Winter Wonderland

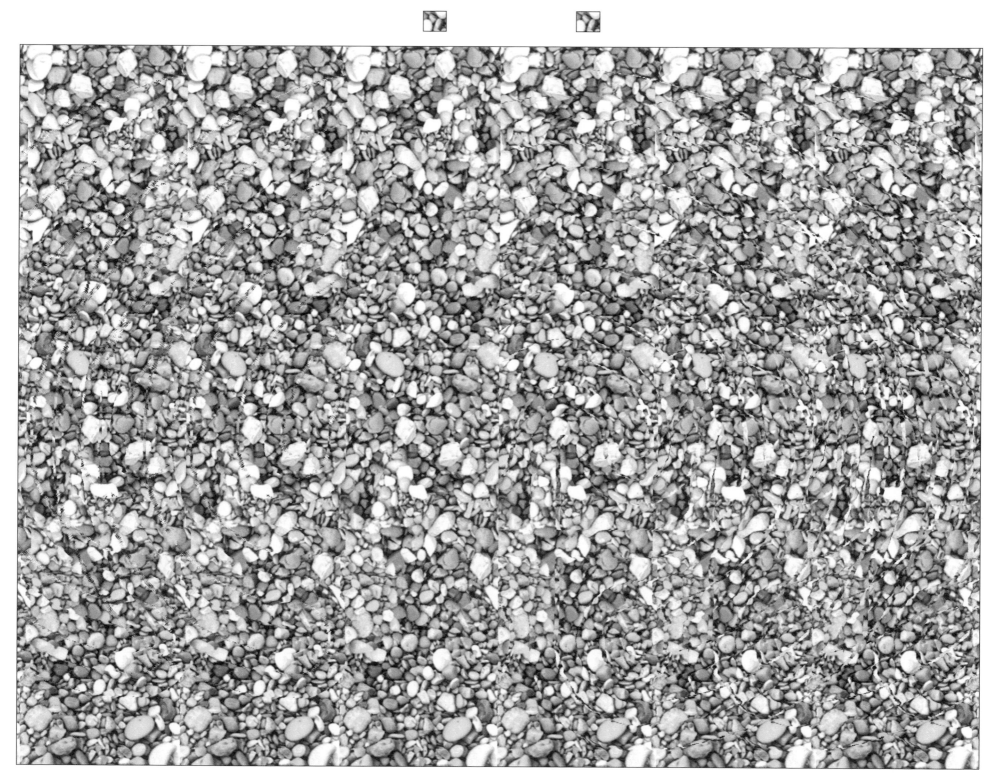

Labyrinth

Magic Eye & Love

Magic Eye images have been proven to help develop visual skills. Did you know viewing Magic Eye images may also evoke feelings of love?.

Vision involves a dynamic relationship between the one that sees and the one who is being seen. Who or what we see changes by virtue of having been seen. Modern physics has proven that even the smallest particles of matter change their behavior when they are being observed. Truly this is a profound observation. Everything changes just through the act of seeing.

When we learn to look with the eyes of love, certain biochemical changes happen in our brain. Here's a brief lesson to help explain some of the reasons we feel "turned on" by love. Basically, it starts with certain chemicals in your brain: dopamine, noradrenaline, and oxytocin, which are neurotransmitters. Neurotransmitters are chemicals that are released from nerve cells, and one of their functions is to turn on other nerve cells that are sensitive to them. This sets up a whole chain reaction. When these nerve cells in the brain are switched on, they in turn trigger chemicals that control everything from hormone release to your mood and blood pressure.

Essentially, dopamine just makes us feel good. Noradrenaline works by triggering the release of adrenaline, the hormone that gets us ready for flight or fight. It's also responsible for that dizzy love feeling, heart palpitations, blushing, and of course those nervous butterflies. You could say that noradrenaline gives us the energy to really enjoy life. Oxytocin, otherwise known as the love hormone, stimulates the desire for connection with another person.

Now, isn't it interesting that these chemicals may be stimulated when you view Magic Eye images? I thought you'd think so. That's probably why we feel that rush of energy and feel so good when we are able to see the hidden images.

So, remember, don't just go looking for love; try to see with love. As you look at the images on the following pages, breathe, relax, smile, and "see" from your heart.

"Seeing is looking with love." ~Helen Keller

"I'm six; my mom is like four hundred. I can see them; she can't. She saw the first man on the moon. I saw Magic Eye. Now we are even."

~Susanna Smith, Colorado Springs, Colorado

"Magic Eye books are excellent! I just bought five books. All the graphics are great. My two sons love them very very much. I hope that those books can be passed down to my grandchildren, great-grandchildren . . . how wonderful!"

~Mai Ju An, Singapore

"Magic Eye's are crazy! They are so fun to show your friends and watch them shove their faces into the books and go 'WOW!! I SEE IT!!' These books are amazing! Thanks Magic Eye for all the laughs!"

~Wallace Kwan, Kent, Washington

"Magic Eye is so cool. I have one in my bathroom at home and have to coax people out of there!"

~Kathie Fugate, Perrysburg, Ohio

"I love Magic Eye calendars. I make sure my husband buys me one every year for Christmas. I have friends at work that come to my desk once a month just to see the new image!"

~Annemarie Ragos, Burlington, New Jersey

"The first time I saw a Magic Eye picture was in the fifth grade. Our class was at lunch, and we were in trouble that day, so we couldn't talk. I had just bought one of the books and I was staring at it for hours on end. Then, suddenly, I saw my first picture, one of a dinosaur. I stood up and yelled, 'I can see it,' and promptly was assigned detention for the day!"

~Adam Sturdivant, Alabaster, Alabama

"My dentist has Magic Eye in his waiting room of his office. Normally I hate going to the dentist, because of, you know, the scraping, the drilling, the whole 'how often do you floss' thing. But now, I love to go to my dentist's office. I just hate leaving his waiting room."

~Chase Briggs, Carrboro, North Carolina

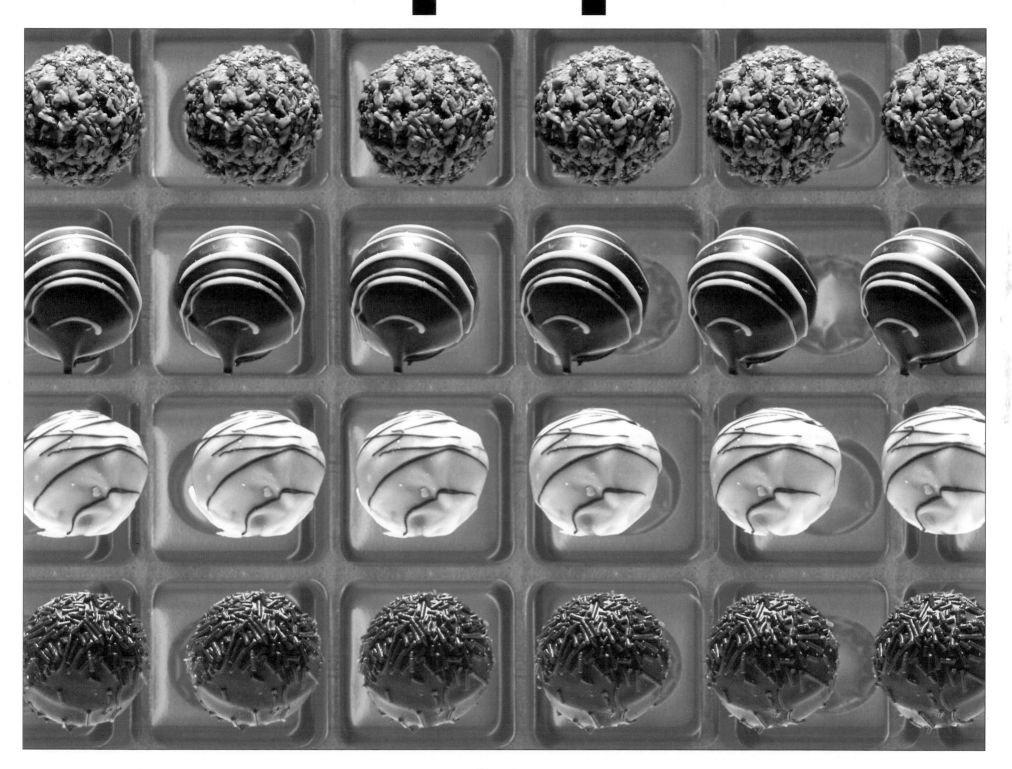

Chocolates

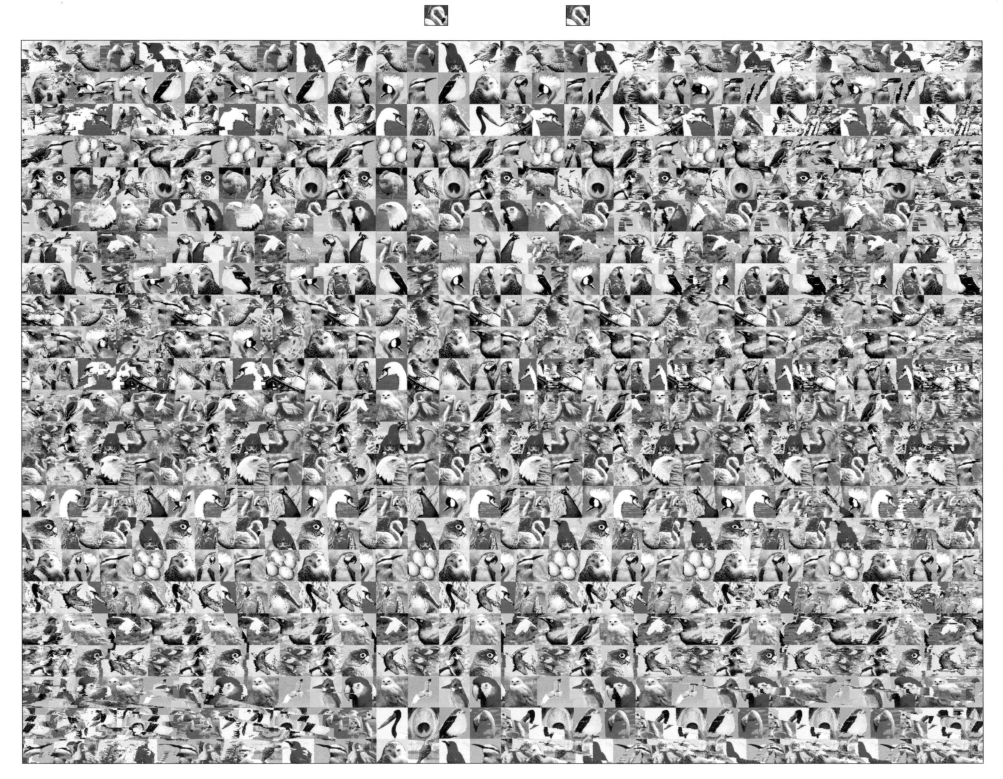

Miracle of Nature

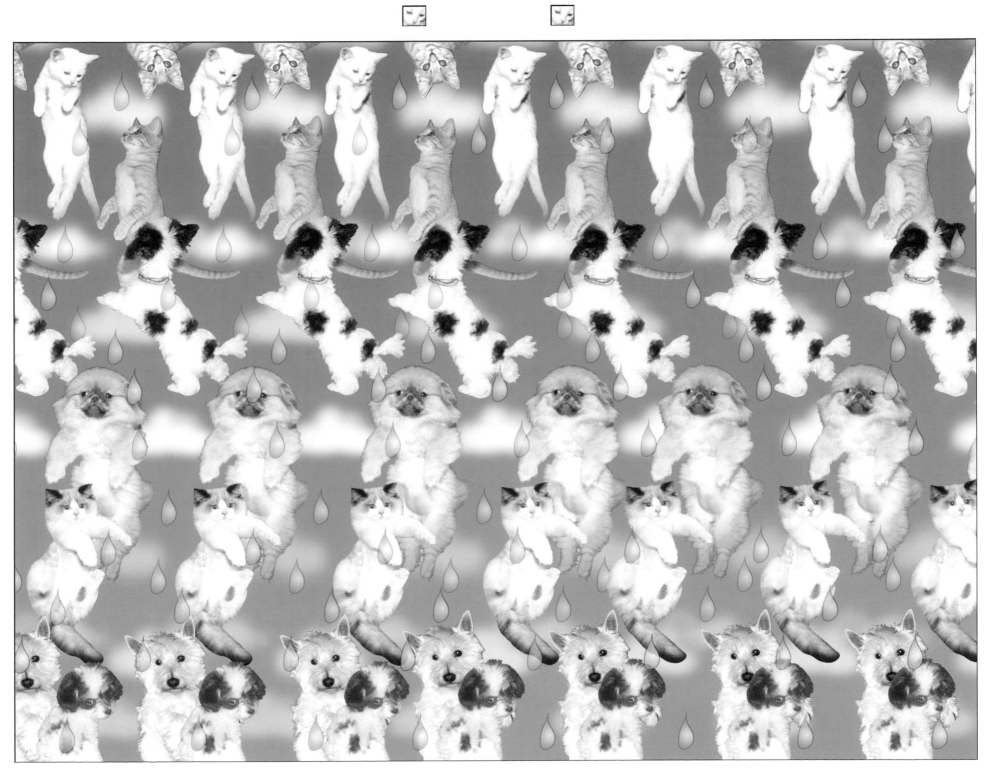

It's Raining Cats and Dogs

Credits & References

SAMUEL A. BERNE, O.D., is a leader in the field of behavioral optometry and vision therapy. He is a fellow in the College of Optometrists in Vision Development and author of *Without Ritalin* and *Creating Your Personal Vision: A Mind-Body Guide for Better Eyesight*.

SUDHIR JONATHAN FOUST, M.A., is the president of Kripalu Yoga Center in Lenox, Massachusetts. Kripalu is the largest center for yoga and holistic health in the United States. As one of Kripalu's senior teachers, Sudhir leads a wide variety of trainings, programs and retreats as well as seminars in the corporate setting. His CD recordings include *The Art of Relaxation, A Touch of Grace: Bamboo Flute Meditations*, and the recently released *Energy Awareness Meditations*, which is produced in conjunction with the Relaxation Company and Simon & Schuster.

JAY LOMBARD, D.O., is assistant clinical professor of neurology at Cornell Medical School and the director of the Brain Behavior Center in Rockland County, New York. He has appeared on *Larry King Live* and NBC News and is a nationally recognized speaker on brain-behavioral-related topics and the author of *Balance Your Brain, Balance Your Life: 28 Days to Feeling Better Than You Ever Have.*

PAUL R. SCHEELE is the author of *PhotoReading, Natural Brilliance* and *Genius Code*. Paul is the founder of Learning Strategies Corporation in Minnetonka, Minnesota.

CATHERINE SWEET, D.C., is an international lecturer, researcher, writer, and teacher of spiritual healing techniques. She has degrees and certifications in chiropractic, chemistry, physics, math, and physical therapy. Dr. Sweet has been involved in parapsychology research with IBM, Yale, and Princeton University. She has been featured in an article in *Harper's Bazaar* magazine concerning new health approaches.

DAVE SHEPPARD studied computer science at the Massachusetts Institute of Technology, built networks at MIT's Media Laboratory, and designed supercomputers at Thinking Machines Corporation. He is currently a freelance computer consultant, designer, and Flash programmer with Sound Visions Consulting.

NATHANIEL ZINSSER, Ph.D., is currently the director of the Performance Enhancement Program at the United States Military Academy's Center for Enhanced Performance. He earned his Ph.D. in sport psychology at the University of Virginia and has since become an A.A.A.S.P. certified consultant and member of the U.S. Olympic Committee's Sport Psychology Registry. Dr. Zinsser also provides sport psychology training for athletes in the U.S. Army's World Class Athlete Program and has conducted workshops in performance enhancement for neurosurgeons, musicians, and management teams. He is the author of *Dear Dr. Psych*, a sport psychology guidebook for youth sport athletes, which won an American Library Association award.

Magic Eye Artists

CHERI SMITH is the president and creative director of Magic Eye Inc. Cheri has always been fascinated with 3D, and has been a 3D photography enthusiast since 1980. She holds a BFA degree from Framingham State College in Framingham, Massachusetts (1979), and attended many postgraduate courses at additional colleges, including the Museum of Fine Arts School and Massachusetts College of Art in Boston. Cheri worked as a graphic designer before becoming a computer graphic instructor. Later she worked as a freelance artist for additional computer graphic and animation studios. Prior to cocreating Magic Eye in 1991, Cheri received several national and international art awards. She loves creating Magic Eye images, and equally loves watching people view them. One of her favorite pastimes is reading e-mail sent by Magic Eye fans.

DAWN ZIMILES received her BFA in sculpture from Parsons School of Design in New York (1991). She then moved to San Francisco where she immersed herself in the computer graphics revolution of the 1990s. Here she worked on numerous multimedia and Web design projects, was a computer graphics instructor, and specialized in creating 3D models and animations. Dawn currently resides in Provincetown, Massachusetts, where her passion for computer technology and art continues to grow. She has been overjoyed to be working for Magic Eye since 2002.

RON LABBE received his BFA from Massachusetts College of Art, Boston, in 1977. Ron became interested in stereo photography in 1980. From 1994 to 1996 Ron created images for Magic Eye as a full-time employee. Currently he works for Magic Eye on a contract basis, as he is dedicated to his own company, Studio 3D. In 2000, Ron was a 3D consultant for the *Sports Illustrated* 3D swimsuit edition.

www.magiceye.com

Our Magic Eye family-oriented Web site receives over 60,000 visitors a week. Fun and informative: Learn the science and history behind Magic Eye images and techniques, enter a contest, view Magic Eye images, laugh at our *joke of the week,* find out *what's new,* and view products in an online mail order store.

If you are interested in licensing a Magic Eye image or having a custom image created, please visit the *advertising and promotions* section of the Web site.

Marc Grossman, O.D., L.Ac. & Vision Works, Inc.

MARC GROSSMAN, doctor of optometry and New York State licensed acupuncturist, also holds degrees in biology and Chinese medicine. He is the coauthor of *Magic Eye: How to See 3D,* published by Andrews McMeel in 1996; *Natural Eye Care: An Encyclopedia* published by Keats in April 1999; *Greater Vision: A Comprehensive Program for Physical, Emotional, and Spiritual Clarity* published by McGraw Hill in 2001; and *Natural Eye Care: A Comprehensive Manual for Practitioners of Oriental Medicine,* published by Vision Works, Inc., in 2002.

Dr. Grossman has helped many people over his 24 years of practice maintain healthy vision and even improve eyesight. He is best described as a developmental/behavioral optometrist, dedicated to helping people with conditions ranging from myopia and dry eyes to potentially vision-threatening diseases as macular degeneration and glaucoma. His combined multidisciplinary approach using nutrition, eye exercises, lifestyle changes, and Chinese medicine provides him with a wide array of tools and approaches to tackle difficult eye problems. This orientation provides the foundation for an integrated approach to vision and its influence on the body, mind, and spirit of each patient.

Dr. Grossman founded the Rye Learning Center in 1980, a multidisciplinary center for learning problems, and more recently in 1996 cofounded Integral Health Associates in New Paltz, New York.

The philosophy of his practice is based on the belief that vision is not static and it need not degenerate. Vision has the ability to improve at any age, and there are practical alternatives for helping vision without resorting to stronger prescriptions for eyeglasses or contact lenses, or submitting to surgery. According to recent scientific and psychological research on the human visual system, emotional and mental stress, childhood issues, and environmental factors have a significant effect on vision. Therefore, to improve vision, the condition as a whole person needs to be addressed including diet, attitude, work, school, environment, physical, and emotional issues.

Dr. Grossman lectures nationally on topics such as Natural Vision Improvement, Psycho-Emotional Aspects of Visual Conditions, Vision and Learning, Holistic Integrative Visual Therapy, Chinese Medicine, and Vision Care. He also teaches workshops for health care professionals, including physical therapists, chiropractors and body workers, social workers, occupational therapists, and other optometrists. Dr. Grossman is a consultant to school systems, rehabilitation centers, and the U.S. Military Academy at West Point.

www.visionworksusa.com

VISION WORKS, INC., is a Web site company cocreated by Dr. Grossman, O.D., L.Ac. Its mission is to help protect and save vision by guiding people along the alternative medicine path with strategies and recommendations based on peer review studies and peer and patient experiences. Any suggestions made are not meant to replace conventional medicine, but instead to complement it with healing approaches supporting and using the body's own natural ability to heal itself.

Vision Works, Inc., offers the following services at its Web site:

- Free eye exercises and vision improvement e-booklet
- Free e-newsletter
- Free telephone and e-mail consultations
- Detailed protocols for over 35 eye diseases
- Food sources for essential nutrients
- Research studies
- Resources
- Self-help suggestions and guidelines

Please visit the Web site for further information.

Beyond 3D
Cover Image

Front End Pages
(Diverge Your Eyes to View)

Page 7   Peace Sign

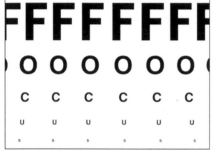

Page 9   3D Eye Chart
(Magic Eye 3D "Floaters")

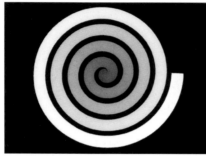

Page 10   Follow the Spiral

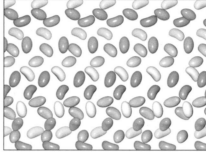

Page 11   Jelly Beans
(Magic Eye 3D "Floaters")

Page 13   Top Left
(Diverge Your Eyes to View)
(Magic Eye 3D "Floaters")

Page 13   Bottom Right
(Converge Your Eyes to View)
(Magic Eye 3D "Floaters")

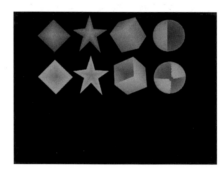

Page 14   Top
(Diverge Your Eyes to View)

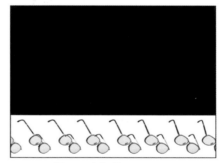

Page 14   Bottom
(Diverge Your Eyes to View)
(Magic Eye 3D "Floaters")

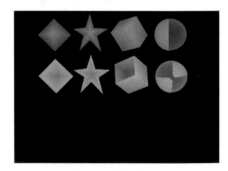

Page 15   Top
(Converge Your Eyes to View)

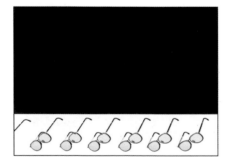

Page 15   Bottom
(Converge Your Eyes to View)
(Magic Eye 3D "Floaters")

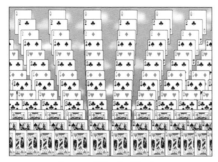

Page 17   Solitaire
(Magic Eye 3D "Floaters")

Page 18   Computer Bugs

Page 19   A Closer View

Page 21 Limitless Potential

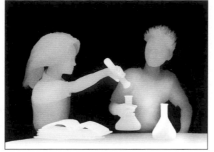

Page 22 Discover the
Unexpected

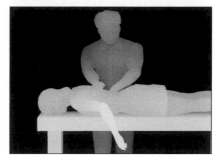

Page 23 Helping Hands

Page 25 Swingers

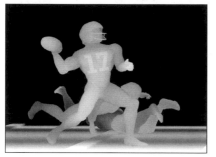

Page 26 Touchdown

Page 27 Pool Sharks

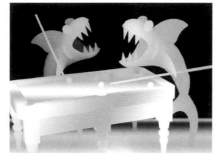

Page 29 Double Helix

Page 30 The Magician

Page 31 Call of the Wild

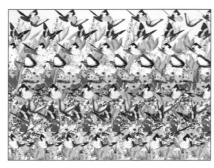

Page 33 Butterfly Promenade
(Magic Eye 3D "Floaters")

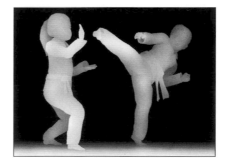

Page 34 Tae Kwon Do

Page 35 Under the Sea

Page 37 Tranquility
(Magic Eye 3D "Floaters")

Page 38 Winter Wonderland

Page 39 Labyrinth

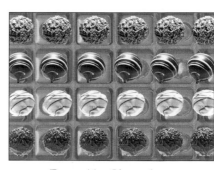

Page 41 Chocolates
(Magic Eye 3D "Floaters")

Page 42 Miracle of Nature

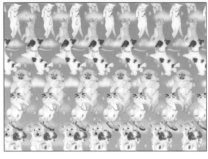

Page 43 It's Raining
Cats and Dogs
(Magic Eye 3D "Floaters")

Back End Pages
(Converge Your Eyes to View)

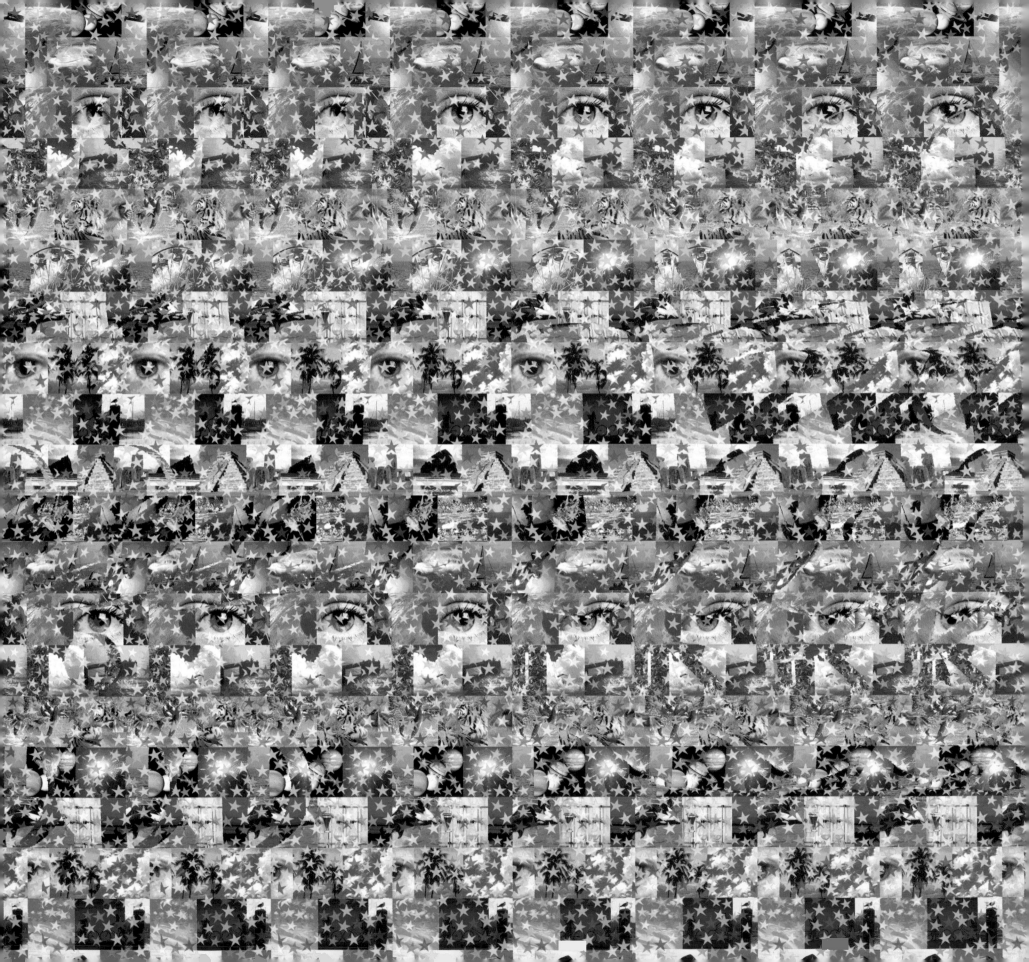